WOMEN'S WORK AND WORDS ALTERING WORLD ORDER

Also by this author

America's Human Connection: Commentary on Us

An Annotated Bibliography of Mary McLeod Bethune's Chicago Defender Columns 1948–1955

Talking Back to Today's News

No Room for Despair: How to Hope in Troubled Times—Mary McLeod Bethune's Cold War, Integration-Era Commentary

Missing News and Views in Paranoid Times

WOMEN'S WORK AND WORDS ALTERING WORLD ORDER

Alternatives to Spin and Inhumanity of Men

DR. CAROLYN LADELLE BENNETT

AUTHOR OF
MISSING NEWS & VIEWS IN PARANOID TIMES

iUniverse, Inc.
New York Lincoln Shanghai

WOMEN'S WORK AND WORDS ALTERING WORLD ORDER
Alternatives to Spin and Inhumanity of Men

iUniverse books may be ordered through booksellers or by contacting:

iUniverse
2021 Pine Lake Road, Suite 100
Lincoln, NE 68512
www.iuniverse.com
1-800-Authors (1-800-288-4677)

Because of the dynamic nature of the Internet, any Web addresses or links contained in this book may have changed since publication and may no longer be valid.

ISBN: 978-0-595-46712-9 (pbk)
ISBN: 978-0-595-70449-1 (cloth)
ISBN: 978-0-595-91008-3 (ebk)

Printed in the United States of America

Front Cover design and interior photo layout by Felix A. Holmes © 2007
NeoZeed Design Rochester New York.

Front cover images

U.S. Representative *Barbara Lee* (Calif.). www.hsph.harvard.edu/.../images/barbara-lee
Former U.S. vice presidential candidate, Native American activist-journalist *Winona
LaDuke* www.tcnj.edu/~studlife/clday/Winona2 Anti-war activist *Cindy Sheehan,* Photo
by Ben Schumin, Creative Commons licensed Former French presidential candidate
Segolene Royal http://www.uncorrelated.com/images/Segolene_Royal and www.renover-
maintenant.org/IMG/jpg/01royal_gr.j Former U.S. Supreme Court Justice *Sandra
Day O'Connor* http://daily.stanford.edu/image/preview/3447?x=225 http://www.
supremecourthistory.org/02_history/subs_current/images_b/006.html.

German Chancellor *Angela Merkel,* http://www.cge.org.uk/12.html [permission 81307]
Jamaican Prime Minister *Portia Simpson-Miller* http://www.jis.gov.jm/
Minister%20Profiles/html/17.html [also http://www.jamaica-gleaner.com/
gleaner/20060226/lead/Images/PNPNewPresidentA20060225rb.JPG]
U.S. Representative *Maxine Waters* (Calif.), Coalition Epic: www.epic.org/.../images/
maxine_waters.jpg Former (2000) U.S. presidential candidate *Monica Moorehead,*
http://www.politics1.com/wwp2k.htm.

Ireland President *Mary McAleese* http://www.gent.ie/downloads/Photos/
Pres%20Mary%20McAleese.zip, http://www.umt.edu/urelations/MainHall/0506/irish-
pres.jpg http://www.gent.ie/images/pres_m_mcaleese.jpg Former U.S. Representative
Juanita Millender-McDonald (Calif., d.), http://tcla.gseis.ucla.edu/rights/features/3/
johnson/millender_sp.html; http://bioguide.congress.gov/.U.S. Supreme Court Justice
Ruth Bader Ginsburg, http://www.supremecourthistory.org/02_history/subs_current/
images_b/006.html [Wikimedia commons] Liberian President *Ellen Johnson-Sirleaf,*
http://www.the-liberian-group.com/; www.un.org/.../afrec/vol19no4/sirleaf.jpg

PEACE
JUSTICE
A BETTER WORLD

Contents

Preface

The Case for New Ethos

Someone suggested labeling *Women's Work and Words* "Feminist Theory" and my answer was: I don't even know what "Feminist Theory" is and I doubt that women covered in this volume see themselves as subjects for feminist theory. I'm no theorist. But if *feminist* refers to someone who believes in full and equal rights for women and that women are eminently capable of changing the world for the better, then, yes, I am a feminist. I am also an independent, a nonpartisan, non ethnocentric, internationalist, and concerned citizen of the world.

My latest work, *Women's Work and Words,* focuses on women without being or intending to be a celebrity notebook. It is a book about world challenges created and exacerbated by a militarist, belligerent, and often a corrupt quality of leadership, which has developed over decades; and a need—answered in these carefully crafted notes and commentary—for a new ethos, new and decidedly different attitudes and approaches to domestic and global affairs.

Recent history tells me the world has suffered a deadly rise in violence perpetrated by one after another U.S. administration (with approval or acquiescence of legislatures) since the 1980s. Washington has engaged in multiple wars and debilitating sanctions against the world's peoples. The Ronald Reagan administration armed space, took hostile actions against the small Caribbean island of Grenada and Lebanon; and sold arms illegally to Iran then used the proceeds to arm opposition to the Nicaraguan government. The George H.W. Bush administration added to the instability in the Middle East by going to war against Iraq, ostensibly on behalf of Kuwait. The William Jefferson Clinton administration further destabilized the Middle East by starving and bombing Iraqis and, in the Balkans, by imposing sanctions against and bombing Belgrade, Yugoslavia. The George W. Bush administration drastically worsened stability in the Middle East by arming just about every nation, neighbors, factions and counter factions in Saudi Arabia, India, Pakistan, Israel, Afghanistan, Iraq, Fatah, Sunnis, Shiites; provoking and threatening Iran, Syria, Lebanon and others; and through its invasion and occupation of Iraq and Afghanistan, causing unparalleled humanitarian crises: massacres and displacement of more than four million people together with border spillovers, mass migrations, not to mention destruction of infrastructures, people's way of life, and widespread fear. This belligerence in U.S. foreign policy—also with negative domestic consequences in crumbling U.S. physical and intellectual infrastructures and institutions—this philosophy of madness was made clear by a 1997 BBC quote of an Iraqi spokesman.

In 1997 European nations (excluding Britain) and some of the permanent members of the United Nations Security Council, Arab countries and others objected strenuously to Clinton's actions against Iraq—as the world in the post-September 11, 2001, era protested George W. Bush's violent aggression. The Iraqi spokesman said the U.S. administration was pursuing "the logic of aggression and show of force instead of resorting to the logic of the age and civilized societies, which is represented by dialogue and negotiations based on international laws, charters and norms, particularly the UN Charter." This is why a new ethos, new thought and action altering world order are essential.

The seeds of *Women's Work and Words* are rooted in my worldview derived from working with and among internationals—the French, the English, Swedes, Africans, Muslims, Arabs, Americans and others—while a volunteer in the early U.S. Peace Corps; and from a maturing sense of women's accomplishments and capabilities obtained while publishing a women-centered newspaper in a southern U.S. military town, and later in scholarly research on women. The seed grew in the 1980s when a friend and founder of the Washington-based Women's Institute for Freedom of the Press said to me in one of many formal and informal talks that people who are wrongheaded or misguided in their actions are not bad people; they just don't have "my information." Dr. Donna Allen also said if you believe important information or history is missing from the public debate, you have a responsibility to supply that information. Indeed. *Women's Work and Words* has intended to do that.

We are a nation and people awash in militarist and corrupt leaders whose services and offices are bought by and sold to private corporate interests: investment and securities, hedge funds, military and sectarian industries, K Street Lobbyists. As former Congresswoman Barbara Jordan said in the late 1970s, "Many [Americans] are distrustful of their leaders, and believe their voices are never heard. Many seek only to satisfy their private wants; to satisfy private interests. But this is the great danger America faces. That we will cease to be one nation and become instead a collection of interest groups: city against suburb, region against region, individual against individual—each seeking to satisfy private wants. If that happens, who then will speak for America? Who then will speak for the common good?"

Women's Work and Words Altering World Order suggests that the United States of America needs new blood. "Everywhere in [America] there are men and women who have real ability and new solutions to offer," said another feminist and presidential candidate (1972) Shirley Chisholm, "but they will never have a chance to serve in public office because they do not have the money to run and win. Meanwhile, candidates who are wealthy to start with, or who are not scrupulous about where they get their financial support, run well-financed campaigns that land them in office—where they become, with few exceptions, exactly the men and women whom we ought not to have representing us."

I am suggesting that the "leader of the free world" needs a woman—but a particular woman—with the intellect and presence of mind and spirit to ponder action while looking to the future, as German Chancellor Angela Merkel suggests; a human-centered person capable of respecting difference and envisioning peaceful cooperation and coexistence with and among nations, as Ireland President Mary McAleese suggests; a woman who is *not* concerned with showing people how tough ("manly," chauvinist, belligerent) she is, or how religious she is, or how fashion-setting her wardrobe.

The United States needs top executive, legislative and judicial leadership which derives its character and courage from the work and words of activists, government and press women, political decision makers and world leaders (past and present) such as Hanan Ashrawi, Shirley Chisholm, Barbara Jordan, Patricia Schroeder, Angela Merkel, Segolene Royal, Fannie Lou Hamer, Lynn Woolsey, Barbara Lee, Juanita Millender-McDonald, Mary McAleese; Nobel Peace Laureates Wangari Maathai and Shirin Ebadi; human rights activists Rachel Corrie, Cindy Sheehan, and Mary Ann Wright; journalists Giuliana Sgrena and Daisy Bates; lawyers Constance Baker Motley and Lani Guinier; and many others covered in my *Notes and Commentary on Nonviolence, Justice, Change Makers, and Peaceful Coexistence.*

Women's Work and Words Altering World Order is the first ever international, multiethnic, multiracial guide, a notebook, seeking to move readers out of the narrow politics of spin and inhumanity of men—and into an altered, better world order as seen thorough a uniquely drawn selection of government, press, and activist women's words and work.

Acknowledgments

The author acknowledges with gratitude permissions granted by Paul Gent of Ireland to use his photograph of Ireland President Mary McAleese (front cover) for one publication only (unlimited print run), as part of a cover collage with credit to the "Photographer Paul Gent, Gent Technologies Ltd, Ireland. www.gent.ie;" by the Conservative Group of Europe for permission (http://cge.org.uk) to use the Angela Merkel image (front cover); by Anthony Arnove of the Permissions Department of Haymarket Books to excerpt lengthy passages from Giuliana Sgrena's book *Friendly Fire: The remarkable story of a journalist kidnaped in Iraq, rescued by an Italian secret service agent, and shot by U.S. forces;* by Julie Snyder of the Carrie Chapman Catt Center for Women & Politics (Iowa State University) to excerpt from the Millender-McDonald and Barbara Jordan speeches; and by Debbie Walsh, Director of the Center for American Women and Politics (Eagleton Institute of Politics, Rutgers, The State University of New Jersey, www.cawp.rutgers.edu) to excerpt from the center's data on women in the U. S. Senate and House of Representatives. Thanks also to Martin Christensen, Copenhagen, Denmark [www.guide-2womenleaders.com], for his extensive, updated documentation of women leaders worldwide and for responding to copyright queries regarding the Monica Moorehead (front cover) image [www.politics1.com/moorehead. jpg] as well to Ron Gunzburger, Publisher of Politics1.com, for confirming that the photo "was one without copyright" (fair use) obtained by Politics1 "from [Moorehead's] campaign site." I am grateful to Nelson of the Solar Navigator Team for confirming fair use of the Angela Merkel image (nelson@solarnavigator.net); to David Monniaux (http://en.wikipedia/org) for clarifying copyright questions related to images appearing on Wikimedia sites; to *Harvard Law Bulletin* Managing Editor Linda Grant for steering me to photo credit sources related to women graduates of Harvard

Law, and to UCLA Professor John Rogers regarding sources related to the Juanita Millender-McDonald image (front cover).

My final acknowledgment is a personal one. To my long-distance English correspondent: a wise, insightful, honest advice-giving colleague in writing, publishing and world concerns, the friend (and novelist) who sees my idealism and, far from being put off by it, cheers me on—to Laura, whose name is my mother's name (or my mother's hers): Thank you for electronic mail conversations from England.

I

Women Crossing Continents Crossing Borders Crossing Colors

Hopelessness is widely available. Giving in to it is an indulgence born of social isolation. We cannot afford surrender to hopelessness.

Women of peace struggled mightily in the George W. Bush years but they mustered the strength to reach out to those hurt most directly by the Bush government's policies. We pledge to do everything within our power to prevent further suffering for you, your children, and all of the Iraqi people, the Women's International League for Peace and Freedom said in its 2003 Women to Women outreach to Iraqi women. "We call on women everywhere to join in nonviolent action to end current military operations and prevent future attacks. We are committed to doing the same. We offer whatever support we can provide, directly to you, in these very dark and dangerous days."

Women's Work and Words in the Spirit of International Women's Day

On International Women's Day, March 8, 2003, women in Glasgow, Scotland, assembled at Bytes and PCs Cybercafe. In Lancashire, England, artists exhibited at Art lounge. Women's Cabaret Night in Somerset, England, featured women performing comedy, drama, dance, and poetry. Edinburgh held ten days of International Women's Day festival. In York, workshop participants discussed the changing role of women. Elgin workshops encouraged women "to learn new skills and talents, and celebrate the roles women play in rural communities." Oxford, England, highlighted women's creativity "through film, music, talks, workshops, art, poetry and

1

exhibitions." They urged women worldwide to continue in struggles for equal pay, for better and affordable child care facilities, for a peaceful world, an end to domestic violence, and against all injustice and violence.

Though newspapers and public radio stations that year as always ignored International Women's Day as well as National Women's History Month in the United States, peace women were acutely aware of the constant need to enlighten and re-enlighten girls and young women (boys and young men) on legitimate ways of knowing and being as evidenced in the ways, work and words of women. Women should be celebrated because their difference makes a substantive difference in the quality of the human condition. Women's International League for Peace and Freedom leader Darien De Lu wrote that International Women's Day and National Women's History Month are important for celebrating "the knowledge that our sisters have always developed means for restoring hope—and even enthusiasm." She said women have done this because they had to. "Women were, and are, the ones left with the children to raise in hopeless situations: after the war, the crop failure, the plague, the flood. Sometimes men were there, still alive, to help. But always, the women have persisted, struggling with their children toward a future. She continued, pointing out that:

> We ... are heirs to this carefully preserved tradition of perseverance—as important in peace and justice work as it is in raising families and holding together communities. These days, hopelessness is ... 'widely available'. Yet to give in to it is a self-indulgent privilege of the well off, born of social isolation. The poor African farmer surveys the losses to a crop caused by some mishap, feels sadness, and does not give up. She does what she can, what she must, to salvage the harvest and feed her family. She cannot afford the luxury of surrendering to hopelessness ... Can we do any less? Take a hand, take a breath—and take action!

International Women's Day was founded by Russian revolutionary Aleksandra Kollontai and German socialist Klara Zetkin more than 90 years ago. The Day's finest hour was women's strike "for bread and peace" led by Russian women at St. Petersburg, March 8, 1917. As years have passed International Women's Day has assumed new global dimensions for women in rich and developing countries, according to articles published by the United Nations. "The growing international women's movement, which has been strengthened by four global United Nations women's conferences, has helped make the commemoration a rallying point for coordinated efforts to demand women's rights and participation in the political and economic process." International Women's Day has become, the UN says, "a time to reflect on progress, to call for change, and to celebrate acts of courage and determination by ordinary women who have played an extraordinary role in the history of women's rights."

Among the most courageous, determined, and effective movers of human progress have been America's black women activists, performing artists, athletes, healers, journalists, educators and public officials. Mary McLeod Bethune (1875–1955) was born poor, a daughter of newly-freed slaves, in the late years of Reconstruction. At the turn of the twentieth century, she built a school that under her leadership grew into a four-year accredited college. The college has stood, educating students, for more than a hundred years. Bethune taught us to build institutions, to network, to fight for access to good work at fair wages. From her position of founding president of Bethune-Cookman College in Daytona Beach, Florida, she championed constitutional and economic rights for women, advised U.S. presidents, and wrote articles that appeared in newspapers and magazines of her day. Some of Bethune's post-World War II columns are compiled in the 2006 publication *No Room for Despair* (Publish America).

Josephine Baker (1906–1975) was among the world's most versatile recording, stage, and screen performers. Refusing to perform before segregated audiences, she taught segregated America to integrate. She integrated Las Vegas nightclubs. She adopted twelve multiethnic, multi-racial children she called the "Rainbow Tribe." She was decorated for her undercover work in the French Resistance during the Second World War.

Marian Anderson (1902–1993) sang "My Lord What a Morning" like no one in the world. Considered the world's greatest contralto, in 1935 Anderson led America to the steps of the District of Columbia's Lincoln Memorial. In 1955 she led African American women into major roles at

New York City's Metropolitan Opera House. Leontyne Price (b. 1927) followed Marian Anderson with Verdi's "Aida" sung like no other opera singer. On the jacket of one album, *Leontyne Price The Ultimate Collection*, the producer aptly crowns her "the prima donna—'a prima donna assoluta' of the international music world." Price was the first African American to sing opera on television. The opera was "Tosca." The year was 1955. The producer was the NBC Opera Company. Price was the state of Mississippi's first to perform before integrated audiences. Her birthplace was Laurel, Mississippi. Her retiring performance in 1985 was "Aida."

Mahalia Jackson's (1911–1972) "He's got the whole world in his hands"—sung for religious and non-religious audiences—is classic. She mainstreamed gospel music on the strength of her international reputation as the greatest gospel music singer in the world. Aretha Franklin (b. 1942) moved seamlessly from sacred to secular commanding world "R-E-S-P-E-C-T" as "Queen of Soul." She was the first woman to enter the Rock and Roll Hall of Fame.

Billie Holiday's (1915–1959) documentation of lynching in her protest song "Strange Fruit" is legendary in capturing a dark side of U.S. life and history. "Lady Day" reigns among the world's unforgettable jazz singers.

Gwendolyn Elizabeth Brooks (1917–2000) was called the "urban poet." She made African American women—and all women who were exposed to her words and work—believe they could win the highest literary prizes. Among African Americans she was the first to win a Pulitzer Prize and the first appointed poet laureate of Illinois.

Cicely Tyson (b. 1933) taught African American women that their repertoire of dramatic roles need not stop with maids and pitiable women. Tyson is a powerful actor who has moved from modeling to theater to meaningful film and television drama. *Sounder* comes to mind. Memorable are *The Autobiography of Miss Jane Pittman*, the Harriet Tubman story titled *A Woman Called Moses* for which she won an Emmy, the film *Fried Green Tomatoes*, and a crusading television series *Sweet Justice*.

Wilma Rudolph (1940–1994) left the world "the heart of a champion" refusing to be beaten by childhood paralysis. At the Olympic Games in Rome in 1958, she set a record by winning three Gold medals—the first for a woman. She led women runners into the New York Athletic Club Meet, the Melrose Games, the Los Angeles Times Games, the Penn Relays, the Drake Relays. In the 1960 Olympic trials she set a world record in the 200 meter. These achievements were a big deal in the early second half of the twentieth century when African Americans were struggling to vote and women were barely two generations past suffrage. Althea Gibson (1927–2003) led black Americans into big league tennis. She won the French Open in 1956 and Wimbledon in 1957 and 1958. New York City in 1958 welcomed her home with its reserved-for-special-achievers ticker tape parade.

Rebecca Lee (1840–1881), Rebecca J. Cole (1846–1922), and Susan Smith McKinney Steward (1847–1918) led black American women into the study and practice of medicine. They were respectively the first, second, and third black women physicians in the United States. Steward was the first black woman to practice medicine in New York State (Hine, Brown and Penn). Joycelyn Elders (b. 1933), a leading Arkansas physician and scholar, led women into national medical practice as the 16th Surgeon General of the United States, the first African American and second woman to head the United States Public Health Service. Elders spoke honestly, courageously on issues and problems related to sex education, tobacco use, national health care, and drug and alcohol abuse.

Charlotte Ray (1850–1911) led women into the practice of law as the first woman black American lawyer. Violette N. Anderson (1882–1937) continued the legacy as the first African American woman to practice before the U.S. Supreme Court, the first to practice in Illinois, and the first woman city prosecutor in Chicago. Constance Baker Motley (1921–2005) continued leading women into American jurisprudence. She was the first federal judge and the first black woman lawyer to argue successfully nine cases before the U.S. Supreme Court.

Sojourner Truth (1797–1883) led women into public oratory and made a name for herself as a powerful orator, abolitionist, and women's rights advocate of the nineteenth century. After the American Civil War she helped people newly freed from slavery and tried to petition Congress to grant land to ex-slaves. Harriet Tubman (circa 1820–1913) freed hundreds of people enslaved in America by leading them from slave states to non-slave states and to Canada. During the American Civil War she was a nurse, a scout, and sometimes a spy for the Union Army. She aided a military campaign that is said to have rescued more than 700 people held in slavery and destroyed millions in Confederate property.

Mary Ann Shadd Cary (1823–1893) led women into journalism as the first black North American woman editor, publisher, and investigative reporter (Hines, and others). She co-founded the newspaper *Provincial Freeman*. She was an abolitionist, an integrationist; a promoter of self-reliance, who criticized Black Southern ministers for failing to teach intellectual growth and self reliance to their parishioners. In the latter half of the 1800s Cary studied law, practiced law, and worked for women's rights and woman suffrage. Ida B. Wells-Barnett (1862–1931) continued the legacy in investigative journalism. As Shadd had used journalism to promote self reliance, Wells used her activist journalism to crusade against lynching. Wells was editor and co-owner of the Memphis newspaper *Free Speech and Headlight*. In the book *A Red Record* is her documentation of lynching in America.

Ella J. Baker (1903–1986) was a great organizer and builder for social justice who laid the ground for future civil rights action. She expanded the NAACP throughout the South and helped create grassroots networks in the 1940s. With activists Bayard Rustin and Stanley Levison, Baker established In Friendship, a group involved in raising funds to support the struggle in the U.S. South. She organized the Southern Christian Leadership Conference and, in the 1950s, managed Crusade for Citizenship, a voter registration drive. Baker founded the Student Nonviolent Coordinating Committee and, in the 1960s, worked with the Mississippi Freedom Democratic Party. Fannie Lou Hamer (1917–1977) founded the Mississippi Freedom Democratic Party when the white Democratic Party of Mississippi refused membership to black Americans. With the MFDP, Hamer (sounds like *name* plus "er") challenged the all-white political candidate pool at the 1964 Democratic Convention. Though she was denied a place on the ballot, Hamer ran for a seat in the U.S. Congress. She led fights against extreme poverty in the black community and for access to voting and to economic assistance. Daisy Bates

(1914–1999) led desegregation efforts in the immediate post-Brown versus Board of Education (U.S. Supreme Court desegregation ruling) period. She counseled, led and encouraged the "Arkansas Nine" (1957) in desegregating Little Rock's Central High School. In the tradition of Cary and Wells, Bates was an activist-journalist and newspaper publisher.

Shirley Chisholm (1924–2005) led black women into top-tier government politics. She was the first black woman (New York, 1968) elected (and reelected) to the Congress of the United States and the first to run (1972) for the U. S. presidency. Chisholm advocated for civil rights, women's rights, and help for the poor. She opposed the Vietnam War. Barbara Jordan (1936–1996) continued black women's lawmaking and oratory legacy. She was the first African-American woman from the South to be elected to the Congress of the United States. As a member of the Texas Senate before going to Congress, she was the first African-American woman (and the first African-American since Reconstruction) to have been elected to the Texas Senate. Carol Moseley Braun (b. 1947) continued leading black women (and all women) into the nation's legislatures and toward the Oval Office. She was the second African-American woman to run for the Office of U.S. President, the first African-American woman senator, and the first woman senator from Illinois.

Through their art, institutions and group activism, black women's legacy has become America's social enlightenment, its strong intellect and moral spirit, its inheritance in progressive thought and being (words and work)—rising from slavery through abolition and woman suffrage, through centuries of movements for human and constitutional rights.

Rider from Wrong Side of Tracks in Olson's *Freedom's Daughters*

Few people are familiar with the Alabama bus rider from the "wrong side of the tracks." Rights leaders and history writers are often vested in their own version of history. They color history to suit their prejudices. Leading players are not always the players who in truth led the action. Women civil rights leaders for example are often omitted from widely published histories—as are women from the "wrong side of the tracks." The erasure of Claudette Colvin and the promotion of a one-woman Rosa Parks legacy is an example of colored civil rights history. But it is important to know Claudette Colvin and all the other women who formed the bedrock of the 1950s civil rights struggle. Not for their own sakes but for the sake of history void of willful error.

The year was 1955. The place: Montgomery, Alabama. Brown versus Board of Education was approaching its first anniversary. Booker T. Washington High School had turned out for the day and a 15-year-old girl was on her way home. She boarded the city bus and sat in one of the middle seats. White-colored passengers began boarding the bus so the bus driver stopped the bus and told the teenager to get up and give her seat to a white-colored passenger. The teenager was a bright young girl: slender, pretty, loquacious, aiming to be a lawyer, Lynne Olson writes in her 2002 book *Freedom's Daughters*.

The girl was familiar with racial humiliation. "Unjust discrimination," Olson calls it. And she had had enough of it. In her history classes she had studied and written papers on the injustice of discrimination. So she refuses to give up her seat as ordered by the bus driver. The driver gets off the bus and calls police officers. The officers board the bus and demand that the young black-colored girl get up, or risk being thrown into jail. She resists: refuses to relinquish her seat to the white-colored passengers.

"No," she says. "I do not have to get up. I paid my fare, so I do not have to get up. It's my constitutional right to sit here just as much as that [white] lady. It's my constitutional right!" This girl showed enormous courage in resisting such force—far more than was required of a woman backed by rights groups.

The police men assault her with epithets: "black bitch," "black whore." They drag her off the bus. Hit her "at least once with a nightstick," Olson reports. She kicks and scratches them. They handcuff her and take her to the city jail where Montgomery authorities charge her with violating city and state segregation laws, with disorderly conduct and resisting arrest. This courageous 15-year-old resister was Claudette Colvin (b. circa 1940)—from the wrong side of the tracks.

Few people have heard of Claudette Colvin because Rosa Parks goes down easier among color-struck, class conscious controllers of message and medium. You will not find Colvin's story in NAACP-approved, mass marketed histories of the U.S. civil rights movement. Not even Darlene Clark Hine's *Black Women in America* tells Colvin's story. Olson's *Freedom's Daughters* does.

Afternoon daylight turns to darkness in Montgomery, Alabama. "By nightfall, news of Claudette Colvin's arrest had electrified Montgomery's black community," Olson writes. Women, in particular, were outraged. Bus riders had been arrested before but this time was different: This was a child! *"She could be my daughter, or your grandbaby, and here were these white cops, manhandling her and dragging her off to jail!* Mixed with the anger, however, was pride in the fifteen-year-old girl who had stood up for her rights ..."

Olson said pent-up rage and resentment spilled out. There was "intense talk in every black neighborhood of boycotts and court battles." Two Alabama State College professors, Jo Ann Robinson and Mary Fair Banks, who also headed the activist Women's Political Council, were exultant. "Finally, they thought, the time had come. They and other women in the WPC did everything they could to stir up debate, to fan the flames of outrage." They made up leaflets, as resistance movements have done throughout the world, "calling for Montgomery blacks to boycott the buses." These activists, Olson reports, "were ready to turn out thousands of copies." A young lawyer was standing by to bring the case against city and state.

But the National Association for the Advancement of Colored People balked. The local chapter's president, E.D. Nixon, put a stop to it by announcing "that Claudette Colvin *would not do* as the focus of a test case." The reasons behind this black man's further discrimination against Colvin were disputed at the time, but Olson reports that Colvin suspected reasons having to do with her being born and bred on the wrong side of the tracks. Colvin suspected Nixon didn't want to use her as plaintiff against Jim Crow because she came from "King Hill, a poor neighborhood once described as 'the forgotten back yard of Montgomery among the railroad tracks, stockyards and junkyards.'" Colvin's "mother was a maid; her father mowed lawns for a living. 'We weren't in the inner circle,' Colvin said." Middle-class blacks "'didn't want us as a role model'." Claudette Colvin stills lives. But when Rosa Parks died in 2005 only British Broadcasting conducted a timely interview with

Claudette Colvin, shedding further light on otherwise censored history. The U.S. press corps obliged the censors by ignoring the BBC interview.

With all due respect to Mrs. Rosa Parks (1913–2005), and to those who prefer censored history, hers was not the bus ride that vitally sparked or jump-started the desegregation or civil rights movement. Her action came after the direct action of a young courageous girl thirty years her junior. Colvin's action and its impact were rubbed out by black male bigotry. Bigotry decree-ing a young activist unacceptable, forcing the rights movement to wait for a fairer representative suited to a particular prejudice—and willfully maintain-ing an error in history—betrays a deep fissure in the movement.

Black women have led in a long line of progressives in the movement for civil rights extending way beyond Parks and Colvin: from Antebellum forward. Olson takes on a big chunk of that history which is not limited to black women. The subtitle of her *Freedom's Daughters* is *The Unsung Heroines of the Civil Rights Movement from 1830 to 1970*.

Freedom's Daughters contains more than two hundred women. Sixty of them are squarely within the civil rights movement. A student with rela-tively uncensored knowledge of U.S. history will be familiar with many of the women but unfamiliar with many more. All students should be familiar with the work and words of these women not only for the historical context of issues and incidents, but for the strength of purpose, dedication, persever-ance, tremendous acts of courage their lives model for later generations.

Some of the unsung civil rights women were

Jo Ann Robinson	Johnnie Carr
Annell Ponder	Virginia Durr
Laurie Pritchett	Annie Devine
Lillian Smith	Diane Nash
Elizabeth Waring	Penny Patch
Gloria Richardson	Mama Dollie Raines
Viola Liuzzo	Casey Hayden
Unita Blackwell	Bernice Johnson Reagon
Mary Fair Burks	

Women who dared to speak out, to educate themselves, to register, to attempt to vote—and those who helped them—suffered threats and unspeakable horrors.

Mississippi 1963 attempted voter registration: On a single night two hundred white supremacists burn almost two hundred crosses in sixty-four counties, Olson writes. "Roaming bands of night riders shot into black homes and bombed black businesses and churches."

Little Rock, Arkansas, 1957: Daisy Bates is helping black students desegregate Central High School: Segregationists target Bates and her newspaper business. Olson writes that Bates was hanged in effigy. "A six-foot gasoline-soaked cross was set afire on her lawn, a note at its base proclaiming: GO BACK TO AFRICA! [SIGNED] KKK ... Night riders fired shots into the house, hurled sticks of dynamite onto the lawn. All the glass in the front of the house was blown out, and steel screens covered the windows." Then a Christian lady shows up at the Bates' door and warns them to stop helping the students trying to desegregate Central High or "'you'll be destroyed—you, your newspaper, your reputation, everything.'" The Christian lady gives Bates until nine o'clock the next morning to answer. The next morning Daisy Bates calls the woman, said to be representing "Southern Christian women," and tells her she is "'truly sorry for her [the Christian lady] and all of her ilk—bigots parading behind the standard of *Christianity*'"—and declares that she "'would not back down.'"

Montgomery, Alabama, 1956: Co-author and lead activist in the Montgomery bus boycott, Alabama State College professor Jo Ann Robinson was sitting in her living room one night talking with a local lawyer and his wife when, according to Olson, "a policeman got out of his squad car in front of [Robinson's] house and hurled a stone through the picture window." Robinson and her guests dove to the floor, Olson writes. Two weeks later Robinson found acid holes in the body of her automobile. Neighbors told her two men in police uniforms had thrown the acid on the car. "In late January 1956 Montgomery police launched a campaign of harassment against drivers, both white and black, who gave rides" to black Americans boycotting buses.

These courageous women of the civil rights movement, these unsung heroines, changed the world working within and across sociologically designated races and colors. Septima Clark was one example. She was a black civil rights activist and citizenship skills teacher whose career had started in Charleston, South Carolina. In the 1940s, Clark became acquainted with Elizabeth Waring, a white woman who was also a civil rights advocate. Later she came to know Waring's husband, Judge Waties Waring. On one occasion when Clark worked with a local YWCA, she invited Elizabeth Waring to give a presentation. This simple act was not going to be easy. It seems Charlestonians hated the judge because he too had become a civil rights advocate. They were opposed to Elizabeth Waring's speaking in their town. Septima Clark refused to back down. Elizabeth Waring came and spoke to the YWCA gathering. The press printed the speech and the temperature rose around Clark (black American) and the Warings (white Americans). "The Warings were subjected to a nonstop barrage of harassment and abuse," Olson writes. "A cross was burned on their lawn, a block of cement hurled through their living room window. The judge received so many threats that he couldn't go anywhere without a bodyguard, and Elizabeth Waring was shoved and jostled on the street."

Black women often suffered alone. The worst of their suffering was dished out by police, jailors and their helpers, the entire penal system. Fannie Lou Hamer was among women who suffered unspeakable horrors and lived to tell her story. Crawford's book *Women in the Civil Rights Movement: Trailblazers and Torchbearers 1941–1965* documents the story of Fannie Lou Hamer's beating at Winona, Mississippi. Olson documents further.

It was a Sunday in 1963. Three women were returning to Mississippi from a citizenship teacher-training session in Charleston, South Carolina. The women were June Johnson, Annell Ponder, and Fannie Lou Hamer. It seems two of the women were demanding their legal rights to desegregate the bus station and the authorities weren't having it. One of the women took down the names of the officers. The officers responded by throwing the women into Winona Jail. But before throwing them into the cell, the jailers beat all three women nearly to death. Hamer's was the most brutal. Olson reports that 15-year-old June Johnson was Billy and fist whipped, stomped, then hit "in the back of the head with a club wrapped in black leather." With "black-jacks and a belt, fists and open palms," these officers of the law beat Ponder "for about ten minutes." Then they came to Hamer. They threw her "face down on a cot and [ordered] a black prisoner to beat her with a blackjack." Then they "brought a second prisoner in to sit on her legs, and when the first man gave in to exhaustion from beating her, the second one started beating her. At one point, her dress started to move up her thighs and as she tried to pull it down, one of the cops yanked it over her head." The other women reported hearing "Hamer's agonized screams."

Teenage civil rights women suffered the horrors of a southwest Georgia jail. In Sumter County less than 50 miles north of Albany, Georgia, young women were participating in civil rights protests and demonstrations. Police subdued more than two hundred participants, using guns, clubs, fists, and cattle prods on them. "[More] than two dozen girls, most of them under fourteen," Olson reports, "were taken to the Lee County stockade. Taken there—and forgotten. Olson continues:

> It was a horror story to end all horror stories. Children who had been burned with cattle prods and bruised from beatings were locked in a cell with a toilet clogged with feces, forced to sleep on a concrete floor slick with urine and other waste, and given cold, rancid hamburgers to eat. The stench was unbearable. Attracted by the waste—flies, gnats, and mosquitoes swarmed through the bars of the screenless, broken windows and feasted on the little girls. Eliza Thomas found a cockroach in her hair one night, and Robertina Freeman spotted a rattlesnake crawling into the cell …

"[The] girls remained in jail for weeks, apparently having fallen through the legal system's cracks" until underground circumstances brought a photographer on the scene. "Peering through the bars, [the photographer] was stunned by what he saw—the garbage, the flies, the stinking, overflowing toilets, but above all those 'beautiful teenage girls' standing and sitting in the middle of that hellhole …"

For all the torture suffered by the younger and older women activists, they remained steadfast in southwestern Georgia as in Mississippi as in Maryland. "Like their sisters in Mississippi," Olson writes, "they never stopped defying white authorities, never gave up the struggle." Nor did a Maryland woman, Gloria Richardson, on the Eastern Shore who had seen her life linked with abolitionist Harriet Tubman. Tubman had been born on a slave plantation on the Eastern Shore. When the 1960s civil rights movement came to Cambridge on the Eastern Shore, Gloria Richardson, "like Tubman, didn't hesitate to take charge."

The story of the civil rights movement cannot be told honestly without the integrated women who worked powerfully and effectively for change. Among them, as Olson points out, were Lillian Smith and her interracial gatherings, Septima Clark and Virginia Durr, Rosa Parks and Virginia Durr, Septima Clark and Elizabeth Waring, Pauli Murray and Eleanor Roosevelt, Mary McLeod Bethune and Eleanor Roosevelt. Olson's *Freedom's Daughters* fills in some answers to questions about who we are, where we've been, what we've accomplished together, and how far we have yet to go in a progressive movement that must include women crossing continents crossing borders crossing colors.

II

Women Refusing to Stand Idly By

Our "sisters have always developed means for restoring hope—and even enthusiasm." Darien De Lu's thoughts from Disarming Despair merit a second reading. Women have done this because they have had to. "Women were, and are, the ones left with the children to raise in hopeless situations: after the war, the crop failure, the plague, the flood. Sometimes men were there, still alive, to help. But always, the women have persisted, struggling with their children toward a future ..." Women have refused to stand idly by.

Women's Words and Work Ending Violence against Children, Women

The rape and ruin of children crosses continents. So great are sex crimes against children that leaders in Japan have labeled sex crimes "terrorism." The second World Congress Against Commercial Sexual Exploitation of Children met in Yokohama, Japan, in late 2001and tried again to face and find ways to end the far-reaching abuse and murder of tens of thousands of children. In the face of this pandemic, not a single print news organization led its front page with a story about the issue or the meeting.

Leading up to the conference, UNICEF's (United Nations Children's Fund) Executive Director Carol Bellamy laid out the problem. She said, "Millions of children throughout the world are being bought and sold like chattel and used as sex slaves." She said the situation constituted "an utterly intolerable violation of children's rights," calling for zero tolerance. Zero tolerance "means ending the trafficking of children, their sale and barter and imprisonment and torture. It means stamping out every horrible facet of the commercial sexual exploitation of children."

A UNICEF report on sexual exploitation said commercial sexual exploitation of children and trafficking are two elements of the more pervasive problem of sexual abuse. Its underlying causes are poverty, gender discrimination, war, organized crime, globalization, greed, traditions and beliefs, family dysfunction, and the drug trade [Through 2007, exploitation of women and children continued to worsen in Iraq and Afghanistan]. "Armed conflict creates special risks of sexual violence and exploitation for women and children. Desperation may force women and children into prostitution. Refugees are vulnerable to demands for sex by camp officials, border guards, police officers, and military personnel. In war-torn Colombia and Sierra Leone, girls as young as twelve have been forced to sexually submit themselves to armed soldiers in order to defend their families." The United Nations Children's Fund reports that women and children subjected to commercial sexual exploitation in 2001 totaled 400,000 in India; 244,000–325,000 in the United States; 200,000 in Thailand; 175,000 in Eastern and Central Europe; 100,000 each in Brazil and Taiwan; and 35,000 in West Africa.

A news article aired by British Broadcasting in 2001 estimated that one million children worldwide—between a quarter and a third of them from Europe and the former Soviet Union—were victims of sexual exploitation. "This ranges from children sold into prostitution, to child pornography on the Internet." The Council of Europe, the article said, estimated that the "U.S. child pornography market alone [was] worth around $3 billion a year." The BBC took the problem seriously enough to headline the issue with links to archived stories detailing the scope of the problem of child sexual abuse from Australia to Africa, North America to Asia and South America to the whole of Europe.

Global: One report talked about an international pedophile ring that started in the United States in 1996. The group called itself Wonderland, membership by invitation only. Their aim was to put hundreds of thousands of pornographic pictures of children online for their customers and members. So what did they do? They initiated potential members by requiring them to first post on their own Web sites "10,000 images of children different from the hundreds of thousands of others already stored in the club's database." Members of this child porn club were described as "educated, skilled individuals who knew how to use encryption to protect the images and defeat law enforcement." They were "male, in their mid 30s or early 40s," with "good 'IT' [informational technology] skills."

United States of America: The University of Pennsylvania released a study showing that as many as 400,000 children are sexually abused in the United States. More than 95 percent of the abusers are known to the victims; children on the streets or homeless children "are exposed to violence, drug abuse, rape, and sometimes murder at the hand of pimps, 'customers' and traffickers." The researchers' data were taken from seventeen U.S. cities and interviews with local law enforcement agencies, child welfare groups, and hundreds of children. A survey of 1,500 U.S. children, ages ten and seventeen years, said a fifth of these children or 19 percent reported unwanted approaches from strangers online. Youngsters most often approached—with talk about sex or invitations to sexual activity—were older teenaged girls.

Australia: An international study found that thousands of Australians involve themselves in the child sex industry. Trafficking in child prostitutes is rising and there is an alarming growth in pedophilia, child pornography, and child sex tours by Australian men overseas.

Europe: The BBC gave another illustration of the "upper crust" peddling in pornography in the world. A British headmaster was imprisoned in Cambodia for filming very young girls performing sexual acts. A Frenchman was imprisoned for child rape during a "sex holiday" in Thailand.

South Africa: A non-governmental organization in South Africa published a report warning that trafficking in children is rising. In 2001 there were roughly 38,000 child prostitutes in South Africa. Girls as young as four were being sold to South Africans and foreigners for sex. Criminal groups engaged in sex slavery extended from South Africa to Bulgaria and Thailand. There are Chinese triads. Even the Russian mafia is involved, the report said. Children from Eastern Europe, Thailand, and China are being transported to South Africa and sold.

Some online agencies are attempting to help. Cyber Tipline (1-800-843-5678) is an online service that claims to help teens and parents avoid getting drawn into the sex trade and sexual abuse situations. "Child-sex tourism is a significant component in the sexual exploitation of children and one that is expanding," the group says on its website. "It involves an individual traveling to a country with the intention of seeking out sex with children." Leadership is needed to end the pandemic, the UNICEF report says. Laws are needed to promote children's well-being. Alternatives must be created to enable children and families to live in dignity. Education is vital because it empowers children to protect themselves. Countries in the West must take the lead in saving the children. Women especially must not stand idly by. Madonna's way is one way.

Madonna, Josephine Baker and Children

Though criticized from the political left, right and colored, Madonna, like Josephine Baker before her, has refused to stand idly by while children are suffering. Malevolence swirled around Madonna Ciccone's adopting a Malawian baby in 2006 as it swirled around Josephine Baker's adoption of her "rainbow" children more than a half century ago. Neither woman let the venom deter her from attempting to save at least some of the children.

Josephine and Madonna are sister-resisters generations removed. They are essential in a man-made, war-torn world that devastates children and threatens the future. Resisters are as levees damming back death to children, displacement and dishonor to millions, despair to generations. When Madonna was adopting a Malawian child and aiding others, children worldwide were suffering. Large numbers of adults, heads of nations, and potential public officials were ignoring their suffering. In 2006 the United Nations, Reuters News Service, and a variety of humanitarian groups had published startling numbers of suffering children.

- Every year close to 11 million children die before the age of five. Mostly they die from "preventable causes."
- Of 100 children born, 30 suffer malnutrition. Seventeen never go to school.
- More than 2 million children worldwide are afflicted with HIV/AIDS, said an International AIDS charity headquartered in London.
- Fourteen percent of adults in Malawi are living with HIV. Ten Malawians an hour, according to estimates, die from AIDS.

- Armed conflict has killed 2 million children, disabled 4–5 million, left 12 million homeless, 1 million orphaned or separated from their parents, and 10 million traumatized in the past decade.

- Up to 10,000 children are killed or maimed by landmines each year.

- Children in at least 68 countries live amid the threat of more than 110 million land mines still lodged in the ground, plus millions of bombs, shells and grenades that failed to detonate.

- More than any other force, the United Nations reports, armed conflict "has transformed the lives of millions of children and women. Children and their families are not just getting caught in the crossfire. Many are being targeted. The key miserable fact of armed conflict in our time is that children suffer most.

- In more than 30 countries children total more than 300,000 soldiers, some as young as eight years old.

- Child soldiers come from impoverished and marginalized groups or individuals separated from their families ... Poverty often drives parents to offer their children for service.

- Eighty percent of an estimated 27 million refugees and 30 million displaced people worldwide are children and women.

- Sex abuse, work and war deny childhood to tens of millions of children.

- Estimations of 218 million children are used for labor, 1.2 million each year are trafficked for labor or sex—millions are in virtual slavery; 100 million women and girls have undergone genital mutilation.

In the face of all this misery, faith-based people, seemingly without concern for the devastation, death and despair among children, saddle their SUVs and modified Humvees and gas guzzle on over to Arkansas' China-based Wal-Mart. What makes the lives of children even more dangerous, a Catholic Relief Services worker told Reuters, "is that no one is hearing about it … The longstanding and invisible nature of the situation has led to an entire generation of children growing up in camps." So along comes an accomplished, high profiled woman in the twenty-first century attempting to be a levee in the storm—standing between criminal neglect and the lives of children.

Singer, songwriter, entrepreneur and actress Madonna not only went through the process of adopting one Malawian child, BBC reports that she is also funding six orphanages through her Raising Malawi foundation and setting up an orphanage for 4,000 children in a village outside Malawi's Capital City Lilongwe. The comparison escapes no one who has read history. This international exotic/erotic singer/dancer raising hackles in the twenty-first century brings to mind an international exotic/erotic singer and dancer of the early twentieth century: Josephine.

It is said that the French enunciated *Josephine* in a way that sounded (felt) like love rising up to meet her in concert halls and theaters where she performed. Josephine Baker was born Freda Josephine McDonald in 1906. In her centenary year (2006), as Madonna returns home to Britain with her adopted Malawian child and is assailed with darts, France celebrates Josephine on her 100th birthday.

Josephine Baker had worked in the French Resistance and integrated soldiers while performing during World War II. When performing in the United States she nudged theaters toward equal seating of people of different races. Beginning in the 1950s, she and her husband settled into a castle in the Southwest of France and started adopting and raising refugee children. Baker didn't stop until she had adopted twelve children of a variety of nationalities, religions, races and ethnic origins. She called them her "experiment in humanity"—A "Rainbow Tribe" that included Asian, European, African and South American children. "I don't want any child to hurt anywhere," she was quoted saying to her husband.

She argued repeatedly with him to rescue more and more children. In this Josephine reveals a critical motivation behind her experiment in humanity: "Children learn to hate. It doesn't come as easily as playing with a doll or a ball." Madonna was quoted as saying her own children found nothing unusual about the Malawian member of their family. But the old guard among U.S. press men, experts, and black and white racialists could not stop themselves from privately, publicly and repeatedly acting out their pathology of irrational racial fears and color prejudices. Madonna understood their problem. "A lot of people have a problem with the fact that I have adopted an African child," she said in an interview, "a child who has a different color skin than I do."

"It ain't gonna hurt you as much as you think," Josephine Baker says while integrating the troops at her performances. "You got room beside you ... You will need a helping hand in the fight. When you hit those beaches, are you going to stop and ask what color it is?"

Josephine Baker and Madonna Louise Ciccone were born of mixed ancestry. Both lost a birth parent. They were Catholics, raised in the Midwest—Madonna in Michigan, Baker in Missouri. They danced their way to New York City before migrating to Europe. Called the Dark Diva, Black Venus and Black Pearl, Josephine, in her day, was the highest earning woman entertainer in Europe. The Guinness Book of Records has reported that Madonna, Queen of Pop—called by the English Madge for "Your Majesty"—is the most successful female recording artist and the highest earning female singer of all time. As Josephine Baker was in her day, Madonna has become a critical resister: a woman standing in the breach between (and drawing attention to) willful ignorance and criminal neglect on the one hand; and the future of the human race on the other. She ventures into humanness to help save the children. She refuses to stand idly by. As did a woman Member of the U.S. Congress whose years were far too few.

Millender-McDonald and Women

In speeches on the floor of the U.S. House of Representatives, colleagues remembered California Congresswoman Juanita Millender-McDonald for having crusaded against violence against women. In one of her own speeches given February 7, 2002, on House floor, Rep. Millender-McDonald had laid out the consequences of violence against women and advised what actions should be taken to end violence against women in the United States and worldwide. "Violence against women is like a terrible disease and, like all diseases, it has devastating effects on many members of our workplaces and our communities," she said.

> Violence against women is like a cancer in our society—hidden from view—but very dangerous. Many women die. Others live— and endure the beatings, the kicking, the broken teeth, and the crushed fingers, the cigarettes stubbed out on their arms and legs and breasts ... We hear of sickening attacks on women and girl children in many countries: We see acid thrown into the faces of young women in Bangladesh. We see honor killings of young women in Pakistan. We see bride burnings in India. We see female infanticide in China and India. We see female genital mutilation in Africa and the Middle East. We see the rape of tiny babies in South Africa ...

In a time when disproportionate federal revenues fund transnational fixers, destroyers, fake re-constructionists and foreign conflicts instead of domestic educational excellence, fair trade and a living-wage economy; when physically and mentally ill soldiers return home from wars with nightmares and no healthcare; when combatants (and often businessmen) all over the world use women as tools of war and commerce, Millender-McDonald's words reveal that she was not one to sit idly by. Her words seem to implore leaders to end aggression as a means of resolving conflict, influencing decisions and actions of governments and factions, or acquiring land or access to other nations' resources. "What can we, as American women, do about this universal violence against women?" she asked.

> At home, we must help to break the cycle. We must not be defeated by violence against women. As friends and neighbors, we must be understanding. We can help women make their own decisions ... For women in other cultures, we, American women,

must draw international attention to their plight. We must publicize—to the widest audience possible—the ghastly atrocities perpetrated against women every minute of the day. We must insist that governments listen to our message and provide the protections to women that all citizens deserve. If we are active citizens, we will be helping all women—American women and the women of the world.

Congresswoman Juanita Millender-McDonald (September 7, 1938, Birmingham, Alabama-April 21, 2007, Carson, California) began her career as a teacher, school administrator and educational writer. She then turned to service in public office, moving from city council to California Legislature to the U.S. House of Representatives (the 110th Congress was her sixth term in office). She never ceased to educate and to advocate for education, women, children, and families—the welfare of human beings. She was an astute, skilled, intelligent, studious politician. Among her most courageous acts in the 1980s, with California Congresswoman Maxine Waters, was working to uncover the truth behind alleged CIA involvement (surrounding the Iran-Contra Scandal) in bringing crack cocaine into South Central Los Angeles. "I think the American people deserve answers," she said. "The mere idea that our government could have, in any way, been involved in the financing or distribution of this horrendous drug is repulsive to me. I believe that it is incumbent on us to investigate these allegations fully and report the findings to the public."

The cause of ending violence against women moves from individual effort to Congress to university institutes and research centers allied with rights organizations. Amnesty International has said violence against women is a violation of human rights that cannot be justified by any political, religious, or cultural claim. Yet men in their lust for unquestioning, absolute power over others have twisted religions, traditions and cultures into sanctioners of violence. A massacre occurred at Fallujah, Iraq. The root of this visceral breach of human rights might be found in chauvinist culture, tradition and religion that individually and collectively subjugate women. Men have used culture and tradition and religion to violate women: to kill them, to force their submission, to drive them into constant fear.

Women in Western New York heard news reports of a 46-year-old male lawyer hiring another man to kill his 26-year-old wife and expecting to get away with it. In California a fertilizer salesman attempted to lie his way out of killing his pregnant wife. These two were prosecuted and sent to prison. Nicole Simpson's murderer, however, was never been brought to justice. In Napa Valley, California, two young women were stabbed to death on the eve of an Election Day. In Wisconsin a man murdered a mother and daughter by drilling gun shots into their heads. An Oregon man repeatedly harassed and threatened his wife, his ex-wife, and his girlfriends. Authorities repeatedly jailed and freed the man. The next girlfriend turned him in for pointing a gun at her, and the authorities finally handed out a stiff penalty. New Year's Day in Sanford, North Carolina, under what newspapers called "suspicious circumstances," a woman was smoking a cigarette on her porch when she was gunned down by a shooter's high-powered rifle. An 18-year-old woman in Biloxi, Mississippi, was murdered by a 25-year-old man. The man had been on probation for kidnapping and robbing another woman and her daughter. In Ciudad Juarez, Mexico (a large border town across the Rio Grande from El Paso, Texas), hundreds of women have disappeared. Some have been found dead in the desert. The governments of the United States and Mexico have been too occupied with *important* matters to find the murderers and stop the killings of women. An Ohio police officer in June 2007 stood accused of murdering his pregnant wife. Two days before Independence Day 2007, the president of the United States threw out the judiciary's conviction and prison sentencing of a member of his administration, a man who had committed perjury (lied under oath) and obstructed justice in a matter which had endangered national security and the life of a woman undercover CIA agent. This same president (first as governor of Texas governor, then as U.S. president) has enthusiastically sanctioned the death penalty for women and the abduction and unconstitutional imprisoning of women and children without probable cause or access to counsel. During four years of hostilities perpetrated against the people of Iraq by this president's government, hundreds of thousands of Iraqis have been killed; four million have been displaced or made refugees. Of those refugees and displaced people 75 percent have been women and children left desperate and prey to sexual assault including rape and murder.

"Violence against women is rooted in a global culture of discrimination which denies women equal rights with men and which legitimizes the appropriation of women's bodies for individual gratification or political ends," Amnesty International reports. "Every year, violence in the home and the community devastates the lives of millions of women." Violence against women is usually close to home—committed by a person intimate with or known by the woman violated or killed. New York City did a study and issued a report titled "Femicide in New York City 1995–2002." The report by the Bureau of Injury Epidemiology in New York's Department of Health said that in 1999 homicide was the second leading cause of death among 15 to 19-year-old and 20 to 24-year-old women in the United States. Amnesty confirmed that without exception "a woman's greatest risk of violence is from someone she knows."

Killers are largely men. According to the New York City report, in 1998 women made up 72 percent (male victims 6 percent) of all victims killed by an intimate or someone close to the victim. Of 1,030 deaths of women classified as homicides by the city's medical examiner in the years under study, 339 were intimate-partner homicides. Of these intimate-partner deaths, 33.9 percent were young women ages 20–29; 51 percent were foreign-born women; 45.7 percent and 33.3 percent were minority women— black women and Hispanic women, respectively. The report concluded that young, foreign-born and minority women "are over-represented among intimate-partner femicide victims." In the period of New York's study homicides decreased. Intimate-partner killings remained steady.

Ignored until recent years is the pervasive, undeterred violence against indigenous women. The head of the Oklahoma-based Spirits of Hope Coalition, an advocacy group, reported that she herself had been the victim of sexual assault three times over. In an April 25, 2007, International *Tribune* article Pauline Musgrove said: "Indian women suffer two and a half times more domestic violence, three and a half times more sexual assaults, and 17 percent will be stalked." Citing figures published by the U.S. Justice Department, Amnesty International reports that "more than one in three American Indian and Alaska Native women would be raped in their lifetime—almost double the national average of 18 percent."

Amnesty positions itself against all abuse against any and all women as life-threatening abuse: "Domestic violence is a violation of a woman's right to physical integrity, to liberty, and all too often, to her right to life itself. When states fail to take the basic steps needed to protect women from domestic violence or allow these crimes to be committed with impunity, states are failing in their obligation to protect women from torture." The United Nations Declaration on the Elimination of Violence against Women defines violence against women as "any act of gender-based violence that results in, or is likely to result in, physical, sexual or psychological harm or suffering to women, including threats of such acts, coercion or arbitrary deprivation of liberty, whether occurring in public or in private life." States are obliged "to exercise due diligence to prevent, investigate and, in accordance with national legislation, punish acts of violence against women, whether those acts are perpetrated by the State or by private persons."

Across the globe women annually take part in programs to alert, raise awareness and rally women and others to the work of ending violence against women. For sixteen days in 2004, stretching from the International Day against Violence through the International Human Rights Day, the New Jersey-based Center for Women's Global Leadership led Activism against Gender Violence. Formed in 1991 the organization publishes a mission of raising awareness about gender-based violence as a human rights issue, strengthening local work around violence against women, establishing links between local and international work to end violence against women, providing forums for organizers to develop and share effective new strategies demonstrating solidarity of world women organizing against violence against women, and creating tools to pressure governments to fulfill promises to eliminate violence against women.

The core cultural-religious-traditional element that prolongs violence against women, says Amnesty International, is the problem of impunity. "Perpetrators of violence against women are rarely held accountable for their acts ... Violence against women is so deeply embedded in society that it often fails to garner public censure and outrage." But women cannot stop with the idea that it's innate to culture. Mililani Trash of the Indigenous World Association says: "By focusing the issue on cultural traditions, the developed Western countries can both demonize certain countries and free themselves from addressing the expanding violence against women." Women must not stand idly by.

III

Women Practicing Journalism under Fire

Nowhere in the world exists a free and unfettered press. But such a press is vital to a free people. A free and unfettered press serves the people and their democracy. In the public interest a free press monitors power: state power and private corporate power. True freedom of the press requires at least three conditions in law and profession. Press freedom must be enshrined in law: within individual nations' constitutions and international law adhered to by all nations and states. A free press must be rigorously protected—not selectively protected but broadly protected, its protection enforced and reinforced without interference of political or corporate bias or any restriction on information gathering in pursuit of truth. Press organizations must scrutinize and employ reporters, writers, producers, editors for their diversity of ideology, race and ethnicity; for their independent thinking; people who are ethical, un-embedded, unaligned and without resolving-door experience with corporate or government power; journalists who are journalists, not propagandists or public relations hacks; people who are unafraid of sourcing widely among widely diverse sources, facts and places in ferreting out a level of truth that is absolutely necessary for a self-governing people.

Free press journalism is not practiced sitting in front of a television screen in a Baghdad hotel or playing stenographer to official government sources or military officers while embedded in their care. Good journalism does not issue from the opinions of focus groups or polls. Such information shifts as the wind blows: according to whims, individual and corporate prejudices, and private wants and interests. Good journalism searches for truth, serves truth, and transmits this truth to the public—for the good of the whole, not for separate classes, tribes or factions. When journalism ends at stenographic parroting of "official" voices or vested interests without in-depth research, broad sourcing, context and analysis (the heart of "reporting")—the result is bad journalism, or something other than journalism. While "feel good" Hollywood endings, happy talk and sappy personal stories might make sweet ambient noise for selling soap, automobiles, beer and anti-depressants, they do not make good journalism in the public interest. The United States' mainly male press corps has for years failed to practice journalism in the public interest. But here and there the world has produced some good women journalists who have labored, often risking their lives in the public interest.

Daisy Bates

Daisy Lee Gatson Bates was among America's civil rights activist journalists who used the press to straighten people's backs and raise human consciousness. She stood down bigotry in the Deep South and urged people to break through their fears and prejudices. The larger context of her work in the 1950s school integration movement in Little Rock, Arkansas, was leadership in representing a long tradition of alternative press practice, the Black Press in America. About her journalism she said: "We brought to the public the conditions of the system in the South. Heretofore when something happened to a Negro and it was difficult to get the facts, reporters went to the white people and took their word for everything. But this time they had to come to me, here. They got the message."

Daisy Bates and her husband, L.C. Bates, opened their newspaper office in the 1940s. They pooled their savings, leased a newspaper plant and opened their press office: the *Arkansas State Press* weekly. The first rub came with their story on police brutality against black men. They had demanded that the city hire black police officers to patrol black neighborhoods. Their editorial position succeeded. And when angry businessmen pulled their advertising, the publishers switched from an advertiser- to a subscriber-driven newspaper and continued publishing for sixteen years, independently in the public interest.

"I was independent," Bates said in an interview for the 1989 book *I Dream a World*. "I didn't have a boss to please. I thought I was strong putting out thirty thousand papers all over the state." Then came what

Arkansans euphemistically call "the Crisis of '57." This caused an interruption in publishing. What had happened was, three years earlier the U.S. Supreme Court had handed down a desegregation decision confirming what Negroes had always known: That separate was inherently unequal and that the South (and North)—under the Constitution—must desegregate. The court ruling was in Brown versus Board of Education. Daisy Bates was in a leadership position in the National Association for the Advancement of Colored People and she took the Court at its word. But Arkansas's Governor Orval Faubus had other ideas. The battle was joined in the Crisis at Little Rock's Central High School. The street battle over desegregation was about to begin. Remembering the segregated school she had attended where students used hand-me-down textbooks, broken down school buildings, non existent materials and equipment; and where they had suffered across-the-tracks bigotry, Bates led nine carefully chosen black high school students into the all-white Central High School so they could have the same chance for equal educational opportunity as the whites. She knew what she was fighting for.

What Governor Faubus was fighting for was his and his constituency's hold on "white supremacy." He ordered the Arkansas National Guard to rid Central High of the Negroes. And U.S. President Dwight D. Eisenhower federalized all the Arkansas National Guard and sent in 1,000 paratroopers from the 101st Airborne Division to enforce federal courts' orders. Daisy Bates, the "Little Rock Nine," the whole State of Arkansas had won. But day after day, especially when the Guard pulled out, Daisy Bates had to accompany the students to Central High and keep their parents engaged (echoes of Harriet Tubman). She counseled and mothered the nine students. Eight of them graduated. "When we took on segregation in the Little Rock schools I don't think we had any big idea that we were gonna win it then," Bates later reflected. "But," echoing the nonviolently fighting Irish, "they were gonna know they had had a fight!"

The battle did not end there. The bigots were not yet ready to move on. Daisy Bates' telephone rang constantly. The threats seemed endless. "They broke the windows with rocks. They burned crosses in the yard all the time. Huge ones. And they set the house on fire … [One] night the police caught some people with guns and ammunition enough to blow the whole town away." Sounds like twenty-first century "terrorism." But Bates worked on, continuing her activism. She recorded her story in her memoir *The Long Shadow of Little Rock*.

After the interruption of publishing in the late 1950s, Bates resumed publishing the *Arkansas State Press* in the 1980s. She later sold the paper. When taking ownership the new editor noted that after fifty-five years the *Arkansas State Press* had become "the most historic African American-directed, owned, and operated newspaper [covering] the entire state of Arkansas." The paper continued "to provide Arkansans with widespread issues, factual information, and progressive ideas. Reaching over 16,000 readers weekly, in 48 of the 50 states and into [Africa]," it continued in the alternative press tradition of "presenting positive images of the black community as well as providing an avenue to reveal topics and issues affecting Arkansans." Daisy Bates died November 4, 1999. She was eighty-four years old. The *Arkansas Democrat-Gazette* editorialized: Daisy Bates' "city, her state and her country can be thankful not only for what she achieved but, just as important, for how she achieved it."

Anna Politkovskaya

The death of Russian journalist Anna Politkovskaya and near death of Italian journalist Giuliana Sgrena, both alternative press journalists, force light on twenty-first century women's great courage practicing good journalism under threat of violence. Despite chauvinist obstructions, these journalists took critical risks in uncovering hidden facts, obtaining untold stories, peeling insight from an under-layer of truth, and bringing solid information to people throughout the world. Anna Politkovskaya was killed in Russia in the fall of 2006. The morning after her death the *Nation* magazine's editor and publisher remembered her as "one of the few remaining independent correspondents [working] for one of the few remaining opposition newspapers ... because the media landscape in Russia [had become] in some ways reminiscent of [the United States] because oligarchs control so many of the papers." Five corporations control the information by owning the press in the United States of America.

Anna Politkovskaya's subject (though not exclusively) was Chechnya, a republic in southwestern Russia where in the1990s more than 100,000 people had died; 400,000 had been forced from their homes during armed conflicts with Russia. The director of Harvard's Women and Public Policy Program, Swanee Hunt, wrote in a February 7, 2007, San Francisco *Chronicle* article that Politkovskaya had been "the world's strongest voice describing the plight of Chechnya's civilian population under military assault by the Russian government since 1994."

The *Independent* in Britain on October 13, 2006, published Politkovskaya's final and incomplete news story, translated by Andrew Osborn, for *Novaya Gazeta*. "After two wars of independence, Russian-backed forces are torturing a whole generation of young Chechens," she wrote, "to try to restore order in the troubled north Caucasus region." The text read like it could have been written for U.S. citizens under the Bush administration. "Dozens of files cross my desk every day," Politkovskaya continued. "They are copies of criminal cases against people jailed for 'terrorism' or refer to people who are still being investigated." She noted that the reason she puts quotation marks around the word *terrorism* is that "the overwhelming majority of these people have been 'fitted up' as terrorists by the authorities. In 2006 the practice of 'fitting up' people as terrorists has supplanted any genuine anti-terrorist struggle. And it has allowed people who are revenge-minded to have their revenge—on so-called potential terrorists." She went on to explain that "Prosecutors and judges are not acting on behalf of the law and they are not interested in punishing the guilty. Instead, they work to political order to make the Kremlin's nice anti-terrorist score sheet look good and cases are cooked up like blinys [narrative poetry or folk history in which facts and sympathies are often at variance with official history] ... This official conveyor belt that turns out 'heartfelt confessions' is great at providing the right statistics about the 'battle against terrorism' in the north Caucasus (where Chechnya is)."

Correctional facilities holding terrorist suspects had been turned into concentration camps for Chechen convicts, she wrote. "Detainees had been subjected to discrimination on an ethnic basis," the majority of whom having been "convicted on trumped-up evidence." The harsh treatment and humiliation caused detainees to "develop a hatred towards everything." Ultimately, she wrote, "An entire army (of ex-convicts) will return to us with their lives in ruins and their understanding of the world around them in ruins too …" Their "hatred … will burst into the open" and to those who "hate the world so much, everyone will seem like an outsider." In a haunting and telling phrase Politkovskaya wondered if "we [are] using the law to fight lawlessness? Or are we trying to match 'their' lawlessness with our own?"

Before joining the independent *Novaya Gazeta*, Anna Politkovskaya had worked for the Soviet newspaper *Izvestiya*. She was born in 1958 and, on October 7, 2006, she died in the line of duty to the public interest.

Women Journalists Killed, Kidnapped, Jailed, Wounded

Journalists' dying in the line of duty has increased dramatically in the past decade. The frequency has been especially troubling in the past six years (2001–2007) as Washington has led attacks against Arab and Muslim nations: particularly Iraq and Afghanistan. Media watch groups report the most dangerous countries for journalists are Iraq, Russia, and Colombia. In March 2007, *Reuters* reported findings of the International News Safety Institute showing that in the decade 1996–2006 eleven hundred journalists and support staff had been killed while practicing journalism. With the U.S.-led invasion of Iraq starting in 2003, the annual rate leaped. In the past ten years (and the numbers are growing daily) a hundred and thirty-eight journalists have been killed in Iraq making it "the most dangerous country for journalists." Eighty-eight were killed in Russia, seventy-two in Colombia, and fifty-five in the Philippines. Reported cases in which journalists have lost their lives have included not only deliberate killings by military forces in war but also assassinations connected with other forms of coverage. *Reuters* reported that journalists targeted or assassinated in countries such as Russia, the Philippines and Mexico "have typically been working on stories about corruption, drug trafficking and other criminal affairs."

On International Women's Day 2006 the international group Reporters without Borders noted that in a decade and a half, thirty-eight women journalists had been killed during or because of their practice of journalism. The list of women harassed, imprisoned, kidnapped and killed in the past few years is stunning. Anna Politkovskaya had been harassed, threatened, and possibly poisoned. Then she was murdered. Below are some of the women journalists who, in the decade 1996–2006, lost their lives practicing in the public interest.

Atwar Bahjat, Al-Arabiya, Iraq, February 2006

Maria Jose Bravo, Nicaragua, 2004

Veronika Cherkasova Minsk, Belarus, 2004

May Chidiac, Lebanese television journalist, mutilated by car bombing, Beirut, 2005

Dolores Guadalupe Garcia Escamilla, radio, Mexico, 2005

Karen Fischer, Deutsche Welle radio, Afghanistan, October 7, 2006

Marlene Garcia-Esperat, Philippines, 2005

Veronica Guerin, Ireland, 1996

Zahra Kazemi, Iranian-Canadian photographer, Iran, 2003

Nadia Nasrat, Iraq, 2003

Duniya Muhiyadin Nur, Somalia, 2005

Kate Peyton, BBC correspondent, Somalia, 2005

Anna Politkovskaya, Russia, harassed in 2004, killed October 7, 2006

Raeda Mohammed Wageh Wazzan, Iraq, kidnapped 2003, killed 2005

Some of the imprisoned or detained women

Mahboubeh Abbasgholizadeh, cyberjournalist, Iran, 2006

Elham Afrotan, Tamadone Hormozgan Weekly, Iran, 2006

Kalshan Al-Bayati, London-based Iraqi correspondent, Iraq, September 18, 2006

Sandra Bakutz, Austrian journalist, Turkey, 2005

Claudia Julieta Duque, Independent Colombian journalist threatened with death, Colombia 2004–2006

Fereshteh Ghazi, cyberjournalist, Iran, 2004

Jennifer Latheef, reporter/photographer Maldives (Islands in Indian Ocean), 2005

Judith Miller, U.S. New York Times reporter, harassed then jailed, United States, 2005

Tatiana Mukakibibi, Rwandan radio producer, Rwanda, 1996

Frezer Negash, Ethiopian Review correspondent, Ethiopia, 2006

Fathimath Nisreen, Sandhaanu online newsletter, Maldives, 2002

Najmeh Oumidparva, weblogger, Iran, 2005

Bhawana Prasain, Majdur Aawaj monthly, Nepal, 2006

Lamasiel Gutierrez Romero, Nueva Prensa Cubana news agency correspondent, Cuba, 2005

Some of the kidnapped women

Florence Aubenas, French daily reporter, Iraq, 2005

Jill Carroll, U.S. Christian Science Monitor reporter, Iraq, 2006 [released]

Marwan Khazaal, Al-Sumariya TV journalist, Iraq, 2006

Giuliana Sgrena, Italian journalist, Iraq, 2005 [released then wounded by "friendly fire"]

Rim Zeid, Al-Sumariya television journalist, Iraq, 2006

The Committee to Protect Journalists says press freedom can be gauged by looking at the number of journalists killed each year and the locations and circumstances under which they were killed. The underlying causes of these deaths are global failures to uphold constitutional rights to free speech and press. The underlying causes are war and partisan (tribal) politics and government policy and corruption. The results are intimidation and murder. Women practicing journalism under fire demonstrates not only their willingness to go it alone; but that the act of going it alone, independently, from the ground, is the means by which a free and unfettered press is preserved.

Press freedom in the public interest is impossible without women. More women must enter and continue in-depth, investigative reporting on war and nonviolence, peace and politics, corruption and human rights, the press and the planet, all in the public interest. The reason is as Anna

Politkovskaya once said: "[The] duty of doctors is to give health to their patients, the duty of the singer to sing—the duty of the journalist is to write what this journalist sees in reality."

Giuliana Sgrena

"'They're attacking us, they're attacking us!' yells the agent. But who is attacking us? Who could it be? We left my abductors twenty minutes ago and they can't possibly have followed us. They could never have entered this American-controlled zone. And I can't imagine it's the Americans spraying us with machine-gun fire. They've surely been alerted to our arrival … And yet, it's them. It's the famous 'friendly fire,' with effects no less devastating than enemy fire," Giuliana Sgrena recalls barely escaping death on an Iraqi road controlled by the *allies*.

In 2005 Italian journalist Giuliana Sgrena was abducted by Iraqis, held for a month, then released. She had been in Fallujah investigating reports of a massacre. Staggering reports that year had been published—in the alternative press. One account was published by the Socialist Worker of Britain. The account was based on interviews and firsthand observations of a physician who had returned to Fallujah with a humanitarian convoy trying to help thousands of refugees camped in horrible conditions on the outskirts of Fallujah. Dr. Salam Ismael relayed horrifying stories of U.S. high crimes against the people of Fallujah. Dr. Ismael said the civilian stories of brutality and massacre prompted the humanitarian group to investigate what had happened in the November 2005 siege of Fallujah. They had heard accounts "of families killed in their houses, of wounded people dragged into the streets and run over by tanks, of a container with the bodies of four hundred and eighty-one civilians inside, of premeditated murder, looting and acts of savagery and cruelty that beggar belief." [The siege of 2005 became the surge in 2007.] He said the city he had visited while working as a physician in April 2004 was in 2005 unrecognizable. The Jolan district of Fallujah, a poor working class area of the city's northwest "seemed to have been singled out for punishment during the second siege," he said. "We moved from house to house, discovering families dead in their beds, or cut down in living rooms or in the kitchen. House after house had furniture smashed and possessions scattered. In some places we found bodies of fighters, dressed in black and with ammunition belts. But in most of the houses, the bodies were of civilians. Many were dressed in housecoats, many of the women were not veiled—meaning there were no men other than family members in the house. There were no weapons, no spent cartridges." Dr. Ismael concludes: "It became clear to us that we were witnessing the aftermath of a massacre, the cold-blooded butchery of helpless and defenceless civilians. Nobody knows how many died. The occupation forces are now bulldozing the neighbourhoods to cover up their crime. What happened in Fallujah was an act of barbarity. The whole world must be told the truth."

Giuliana Sgrena too had interviewed civilians in Fallujah in search of the truth of what had happened there. She was heading home to relay her findings to the world. On the night of her release she was traveling on a road leading to the Baghdad airport. Accompanying her were Italian secret service agents. U.S. soldiers fired on the three of them. The attack left senior secret service agent Nicola Calipari dead and Giuliana Sgrena close to death from tank-mounted fire power. Her shoulder was shattered, her lung punctured.

Sgrena documented the incident in *Friendly Fire: The remarkable story of a journalist kidnaped in Iraq, rescued by an Italian secret service agent, and shot by U.S. forces.* The book was released in 2006 in the United States. In *Friendly Fire* Sgrena says the incident on a road that would have taken her to an airport and a plane destined for her homeland brought her up hard against "the real origins of the current situation in Iraq: the war." This story is important not only because of Sgrena's near-death injuries and the death of the secret service agent accompanying her, but because the incident of "friendly fire" lays bare war's blind (or worse, deliberate) lawlessness. War is an act of lawlessness that not only fails to distinguish friend from foe but it deliberately sets out to silence all possibility of letting truth escape the theater of war and its lawlessness. In this war there have been untold numbers of friendly fire incidents resulting from blind attacks failing to distinguish friend from foe ultimately reaching way beyond shattered shoulders and murdered allies. Friendly fire occurs when everybody is the enemy and no one, especially a bearer of un-propagandized truth, escapes unscathed. "In Baghdad," Sgrena reports, "anything can happen with the most complete impunity."

Truth is the bloodiest casualty of a "war of liberation" unmasked as war of raw aggression turned perpetual occupation: Perpetual War. A war in which un-embedded journalists such as Giuliana Sgrena are suspect on all sides: suspected of being collaborators or spies, "terrorists" or terrorist sympathizers. In a world of perpetual war, conflict and corruption, the press worldwide is under siege and its workers in the public interest are under threat and silenced outright. Reporters without Borders published in June 2007 what was then the current list of journalists killed, arrested, and threatened in 2007 in the line of duty.

2007 Journalists Killed: 42
U.S.-occupied Iraq: 26

May 30, 2007—Nizar Al-Radhi, Aswat Al-Irak

May 29, 2007—Abdel-Rahmane Al-Issaoui, Independant May 28, 2007—Mahmoud Hassib Al-Kassab, Al-Hawadith

May 26, 2007—Aidan Abdallah Al-Jamiji, Kirkouk TV

May 20, 2007—Ali Khalil, Al-Zaman

May 17, 2007—Saif Laith Yousuf, ABC May 17, 2007—Alaa Uldeen Aziz, ABC

May 9, 2007—Raad Mutasha al-Issawi, Al-Iraq Al-Ghad, Al-Raad

May 9, 2007—Nibras Abdel-Razak Obaid, Al-Iraq Al-Ghad, Al-Raad

May 9, 2007—Imad Obaid, Al-Iraq Al-Ghad, Al-Raad

May 6, 2007—Dmitry Chebotayev, Newsweek

April 12, 2007—Iman Yussef Abdallah, The sound of Mossul

April 9, 2007—Othman al-Mashhadani, Al-Watan

April 6, 2007—Khamail Khalaf, Radio Free Europe

April 5, 2007—Thaer Ahmed Jabr, Baghdad TV

March 19, 2007—Hamid al-Duleimi, al-Nahrain

March 16, 2007—Hussein al Jaburi, al-Safir

March 7, 2007—Yussef Sabri, Biladi TV

March 4, 2007—Mohan Hussein al-Dhahr, al-Mishrak

March 3, 2007—Jamal Riyah Al Zoubaidi, As-Safir

February 20, 2007—Abderrazak Hashim Al-Khakani, Jumhuriyat Al Iraq

February 19, 2007—Hussein Al Zubaydi, al-Ahali

January 28, 2007—Munjid Al-Tumaimi, Freelance photographer

January 15, 2007—Falah Khalaf Al Diyali, Al Saha

January 14, 2007—Yassin Aid Assef, Al Sabah January 12, 2007—Khoudr Younes al-Obaidi, Freelance

U.S.-armed Pakistan: 2

June 2, 2007—Noor Hakim, Urdu-language daily Pakistan and vice-president of the Tribal Union of Journalists

April 28, 2007—Mehboob Khan, Free-lance

U.S.-occupied Afghanistan: 1

April 8, 2007—Adjmal Nashqbandi, La Repubblica

Brazil: 1

May 5, 2007—Luiz Carlos Barbom Filho, Jornal do porto

China: 1

January 11, 2007—Lan Chengzhang, Zhongguo Maoyi Bao

Haïti: 1

January 19, 2007—Jean-Rémy Badiau, freelance photographer

Mexico: 2

April 16, 2007—Saúl Martínez Ortega, Diario de Agua Prieta, Interdiario

April 6, 2007—Amado Ramírez, Radiorama Acapulco, Televisa

Palestinian Authority: 1

May 13, 2007—Suleyman Al-Aashi, Filistin

Peru: 1

March 16, 2007—Miguel Pérez Julca, Radio Exitos

U.S.-attacked Somalia: 4

May 15, 2007—Abshir Ali Gabra, Radio Johwar, Radio Quran Kariim

May 15, 2007—Ahmed Hassan, Radio Johwar, Somalia Broadcasting Corporation

May 5, 2007—Mohammed Abdullahi Khalif, Radio Voice of Peace

February 16, 2007—Ali Mohammed Omar, Radio Warsan

Turkey: 1

January 19, 2007—Hrant Dink, Agos Zimbabwe: 1

March 31, 2007—Edward Chikomba, Freelance

2007 Media assistants killed: 8

Media assistants imprisoned: 6

Journalists imprisoned: 125

Cyber-dissidents imprisoned: 68

Journalists Killed in Previous Half Decade:

Killed in 2006: 84

Killed in 2005: 63

Killed in 2004: 62

Killed in 2003: 40

Killed in 2002: 25

"No one wants witnesses," Sgrena writes: "neither the occupiers, who went to war on a pretext built of lies, nor the occupied, who fear any revelations about themselves as they fight the occupation. Information becomes the enemy, another victim of war. Today, in an era when technology allows us to disseminate information in real time, independent news can be dangerous. Therefore, journalists are also potential enemies …" The bravery of this un-embedded journalist who, before her abduction, had covered stories from Somalia to Algeria, Palestine to Afghanistan, including Iraq, cannot be overstated. Yet she admits in the book that she miscalculated the ruthlessness driving this particular war. "Evidently—and this is my one regret," she writes: "I had not calculated how far the degeneration of war could reach …

"The abduction was the proof that the armed resistance (or at least some of its factions) is not interested in having a relationship with the outside world, given that it treats all foreigners as enemies. It no longer makes any distinction between the soldiers occupying the country, contractors waging a dirty war, humanitarian workers working side by side with the most needy, and journalists who want to report on a different reality than that seen by embedded reporters through the filter (or censor) of military command."

The resisters in Iraq clearly want the "foreigners" off their land and a journalist such as Sgrena is indistinguishable on the ground of war. Feeling, as she puts it, "a prisoner and victim of a war that I, like millions of others, have always opposed—futilely. And now I feel doubly defeated."

But before the war Iraqis were not hostile to foreigners on their land. There exists a before-the-war and an after-war attitude based on drastically changed conditions. Sgrena reflects on an article she had written before the war describing Iraqis as "gentle but not servile; proud but not arrogant." She says, "It is we who are barbarous compared to their civilization, born in Mesopotamia six thousand years ago, which has left its indelible traces on the history of humanity." After the U.S.-led invasion, conditions changed, as did Iraqis. Now, "I see hate in their eyes. They are no longer gentle. They are still proud, but also violent, and they are abducting me." Detailing Iraqi lives as she had observed living among Iraqis in war, Sgrena says they too are caught between life and death, basic security a daily nightmare. She continues at length:

> Fear of being hit by an exploding car bomb, or finished off by a spray of American machine gun fire because of one wrong move when a military convoy rumbles into the hellish traffic of Baghdad, or simply because you pass in front of a base or a U.S. checkpoint at the wrong time. Fear of being abducted ...: thousands of Iraqis are taken hostage ... Those who work with foreigners are often among the abductees, since they're believed to be 'collaborators'; the same goes for government workers, or employees of almost any institution at all ... Not even the youngest children are spared ... For this reason, children are shut up in their houses by their parents. They can no longer play in the streets or yards ... [Abduction] for girls, even the very young, often means rape.

Based on her extensive experience covering the conflict and with a deep interest in peace, Sgrena acknowledges the importance of resistance to occupation yet condemns war, whether as hostage taking, as ground fire, or as air strikes. Her advice is withdrawal and real reconstruction. Though withdrawal will not bring peace immediately, she says, and factional clashes will likely intensify, withdrawal will take away "the alibi of those using violence to fight the occupiers, and above all, of the terrorists, who are not interested in the liberation of Iraq, but are using the Iraqi territory to fight their Jihad (holy war), ... against the Shiite 'traitors' (as they are considered by Sunni fundamentalists)." In its current war-ravaged condition, Sgrena writes, "Iraq cannot be abandoned." Once the country regains its sovereignty, "the Iraqis must be helped to rebuild their country, a task that cannot be done with tanks and Apache helicopters."

Another veteran woman journalist, an American, was wounded by her own paper, but not bowed. She left her post at the Los Angeles *Times* in the spring of 2007. In an article in the Huffington *Post* Nancy Cleeland reflected on why she was leaving the *Times*. She said news organizations' shallowness is failing the public interest. She said her news organization had become "increasingly anti-union in its editorial policy, [celebrity oriented] ... and crime-focused in its news coverage, [ignoring] the economic discontent that is clearly reflected in ethnic publications." The consequence, she said, is that "hundreds of other mid-career journalists are walking away from media institutions across the country ... looking for other ways to tell the stories [they] care about."

The U.S. press has become one male voice indistinguishable. But democracy cannot survive without women journalists like Bates and Politkovskaya and Sgrena telling substantive stories they care about—and the public must care about.

In a constitutional democracy the Constitution must stand between the people, the individual, the minority; and the onerous powers of oligarchies and the State. Constitutional amendments including the First Amendment are not intended to serve corporate power. Contrary to President George W. Bush's assertion that the U.S. government is *his* government, it is the Constitution that creates government, all branches of it, and sets out the rules under which government is to serve the people: "establish justice, insure domestic tranquility, provide for the common defense (not invade sovereign nations), promote the general welfare." Public officials are sworn to uphold the Constitution and the press must hold their feet to the fire of that sworn duty. The long history—some might say deterioration—of the press in the United States and around the world has demonstrated that an independent Fourth Estate cannot exist and will not do its duty without Women of the Press practicing their profession under fire.

IV

Women Judges, Lawyers upholding United States Constitution

Diana Gribbon Motz, Ruth Bader Ginsburg, Gladys Kessler

By the spring of 2007 the Bush administration had committed a long line of constitutional breaches in what was commonly termed "global war on terror." The government had imprisoned hundreds of civilians, including U.S. citizens and other nationals, without publishing cause or charge or producing evidence of wrongdoing. The case of U.S. resident Saleh Kahlah al-Marri's open-ended imprisonment without charge came before the U.S. Court of Appeals for the Fourth Circuit. And Judge Diana Gribbon Motz capsulized the deep breach committed by the administration: "To sanction such a presidential authority to order the military to seize and indefinitely detain civilians ...," a June 12 Washington *Post* article quoted Judge Motz, "would have disastrous consequences for the constitution—and the country."

Another branch of government that spring sided against working women. But Justice Ruth Bader Ginsburg, the lone woman on the U.S. Supreme Court, led a powerful dissent in a case of wage discrimination against women. The case was Lilly M. Ledbetter, Petitioner, versus the Good Year Tire & Rubber Company Inc. Ledbetter had charged the company with wage discrimination and the majority on the Supreme Court had ruled that the statute of limitations had run out for filing a pay discrimination claim. Understanding working women and the often insidious nature of discrimination against women and the tendency of the good old boys to shut women out, Justice Ginsburg opposed the statute of limitations claim and charged the Court with failing to uphold the intent of Congress in Title VII. "The Court's insistence on immediate contest overlooks common characteristics of pay discrimination," Justice Ginsburg wrote in her dissent.

> Pay disparities often occur, as they did in Ledbetter's case, in small increments; cause to suspect that discrimination is at work develops only over time. Comparative pay information, moreover, is often hidden from the employee's view. Employers may keep under wraps the pay differentials maintained among supervisors, no less the reasons for those differentials. Small initial discrepancies may not be seen as meet for a federal case, particularly when the employee, trying to succeed in a nontraditional environment, is averse to making waves ... Pay disparities are thus significantly different from adverse actions such as termination, failure to promote ... or refusal to hire, all involving fully communicated discrete acts, easy to identify as discriminatory ... [Ledbetter's] initial readiness to give her employer the benefit of the doubt should not preclude her from later challenging the then current and continuing payment of a wage depressed on account of her sex ... Our precedent suggests, and lower courts have overwhelmingly held, that the unlawful practice is the current payment of salaries infected by gender-based (or race-based) discrimination, a practice that occurs whenever a paycheck delivers less to a woman than to a similarly situated man.

While not carrying the majority on the U.S. Supreme Court, Justice Ginsburg's dissent will on review influence later court deliberations on wage discrimination against women. "[Women's] very presence in the judiciary," D.C. Superior Court Judge Gladys Kessler noted in an interview with the Harvard Law School Bulletin, "has helped the system acknowledge the realities of women's lives. Women have a responsibility to make a difference in the legal system and the administration of justice." And dozens of American women in law and justice have made substantial differences.

Constance Baker Motley (1921–2005)

Cases tried by Constance Baker Motley against Mississippi, Alabama and Georgia universities and against South Carolina's Clemson College in the 1960s changed minds. The cases changed legal and social landscapes. Motley's success in these cases as documented in *Black Women in America* resulted in sea changes: James Meredith's rise to American hero; Charlayne Hunter-Gault and Hamilton Holmes's impetus in dragging Georgia kicking and screaming into a new century; Alabama Governor George Wallace's surrender of his public resistance to desegregation; and South Carolina's ultimate celebration of its native son: Clemson graduate Harvey Gantt, who rose to high elective office as Charlotte, North Carolina's, mayor and viable candidate for higher state and federal office.

In times when racism gallops prime time into American homes via satellite-channeled wide screen electronics, times when powerful people look into the faces of racism's result and respond with egregious vitriol against colored people, it is time for colored people themselves to reflect, more seriously and differently, upon who they are and, because of who they are, what constitutes the nature of their duty in the world. In a lifetime as judge, lawyer and politician, Constance Baker Motley lifted the movement for justice under law and led the charge for change in the United States of America. As we grieved her passing in 2005, no doubt in her later years she had grieved the backward trend in civil rights and equal justice. America has slipped dangerously backward. But a brief look into Judge Motley's background reminds of the individual's duty to push America forward.

Constance Baker Motley endured racism and persevered. When President Lyndon Johnson nominated her for a seat on the U.S. Court of Appeals for the Second Circuit, the racism was so strong from the lips and power of Mississippi *Dixiecrat* (Senator) James Eastland that Johnson backed down, withdrew the nomination. Along with Eastland's vitriol, racists and sexists and bigots of all stripes had stood in the way of her work as a lawyer, a judge, and as Borough President of Manhattan (New York City). Taxi drivers refused to stop for her and letter writers sent hate mail. But she persevered.

Historian and professor of African-American studies Nancy MacLean writing in a 2002 issue of the Journal of Women's History urged other historians to take a serious look into the life and work—indeed the character—of Constance Baker Motley. MacLean suggests looking into how an accomplished woman professional was treated by her follow Americans. Look at the way white supremacist (irrational) judges, politicians, journalists and ordinary men reacted. MacLean wrote: "Senate Judiciary Committee Chairman James Eastland conducted a seven-month campaign which at first successfully stopped an appointment to the federal bench of a highly qualified African American woman. Southern judges refused to address her in court. Mississippi newspapers referred to her as 'the Motley woman.' Motley sustained 'excruciating and shockingly trivial' northern bias against her as an African American, as a woman and particularly as a black woman—which means her detractors were both white people and black men."

MacLean suggests looking at the connection Motley recognized between grassroots activism and legal change, legal change and grassroots activism. "Historians need to understand better how legal change was both enabled by grassroots activism and in turn shaped by such activism." Motley's life makes clear the interdependence of the two tracks, MacLean observes. In her work as an attorney with the NAACP Legal Defense and Education Fund, Motley worked on almost every civil rights case brought to trial between 1945 and 1965, MacLean writes; the "attorneys' legal victories [in these cases] inspired local leaders to more ambitious plans for change." A 1951 victory against the University of Texas law school led black parents and NAACP branches to push for desegregating primary and secondary schools. The result was Brown v. Board of Education of Topeka. Motley and others' collective victories at court "shored up the 1963 Birmingham crusade led by Martin Luther King Jr. and the Southern Christian Leadership Conference."

Change requires legal challenge and continuous grassroots activism. The need for change does not end with political promises or the appearance of gains. Motley's life teaches the importance of self awareness and the individual's responsibility to use life and position to extend equal justice under law. Lead by example. MacLean quotes Motley saying in her autobiography *Equal Justice under Law,* "'I also coincided with history, and I have never lost sight of that fact.'" MacLean continues:

> This deep awareness of her life's context along with her abiding commitment to fairness made Motley's practice on the federal bench distinctive. Not only did she decide a leading employment rights case for women, Ludtke v. Kuhn, that in 1978 gave women sportswriters access to the New York Yankee's locker room ... She also regularly selected women and minority law clerks [as Eleanor Roosevelt did with women of the press] when doing so was unusual. In turn, her presence on the bench prompted law firms and government agencies to use minority and women attorneys in her court ...

Constance Baker Motley was born of British West Indian parents who had immigrated to the New England home of Yale University. Motley traced her roots to Nevis, an English West Indian island in the Caribbean where slavery had been abolished in 1833—thirty years before slavery was outlawed in the United States of America. In Nevis her mother was a seamstress, her father a cobbler. They moved to the United States just after the turn of the twentieth century. Constance Baker was born the year after ratification of Woman Suffrage (1920), the Nineteenth Amendment to the United States Constitution.

In her autobiography Motley writes: "I grew up in a lower-middle-class household where my father was head of the house ... West Indian men (particularly those from the British islands) wanted to demonstrate, always, that they were as capable as any man." Her mother taught her American responsibility: "My mother was a tolerant, peace-seeking person, who did not have strong views on race and never disparaged any ethnic group," Motley writes. "She understood well America's basic creed of equality."

With mixed heritage—English, West Indian, American, African American—Motley began her undergraduate work at Fisk University. Then realizing her need to integrate into a larger society, she transferred to New York University. She graduated. Then entered and graduated from Columbia University law school. From the1940s through the 1990s

Motley's career moved her from practicing law through three branches of government: associate counsel for the New York-based NAACP Legal Defense and Education Fund, New York state senator, Manhattan Borough President, U.S. District Court judge, Chief Judge, and Senior Judge.

Constance Baker Motley said she learned from her parents an uncompromising sense of self respect and the importance of advancing the cause of justice for people who had been denied justice. Motley left America a legacy rooted in a fertile ground of accomplishments born of self knowledge, preparedness, duty, responsibility and activism.

Lani Guinier Empowered by Motley

Professor Lani Guinier studied law at Yale in the 1970s where she was "present but invisible." The reason for this, she told an interviewer, was she felt stung by the greeting of her corporations law professor. The greeting was always the same greeting: "Good morning, gentlemen." And, ladies, you "should not feel excluded by this greeting." Guinier says she remained silent for the duration of the course. She made it through Yale law and attributes her success in getting through Yale and other situations to Constance Baker Motley.

Guinier had observed Motley at work long before she began studies at Yale. In 1962 when she was 12 years old she had watched a televised report showing the NAACP's Legal Defense Fund counsel Constance Baker Motley escorting James Meredith into the University of Mississippi. Guinier said to herself: "I can do that, I can be a woman lawyer in the cause of civil rights." From 1981 through 1988 Guinier was a counsel for the Legal Defense Fund. She helped win major voting rights victories in Alabama and other southern states. In 2007 Professor Lani Guinier was still teaching law at Harvard University.

Words and Work: Women Jurists, Lawyers from Harvard

Charlotte Armstrong (Harvard Law 1953): "You just put one foot in front of another and then it turns out that you are a trailblazer."

Frederica Brenneman (Harvard Law 1953): Besides her judicial work she is known for having been actively involved "in training judges, social workers, lawyers and others to respond to child abuse." Until 1967 she had been the second woman in Connecticut judicial history to have been appointed juvenile court judge.

Ruth Abrams (Harvard Law 1956): Well-known for supporting gender equity and minority rights. Reflecting on her opinions in interviews she characterized them as "putting out a helping hand to people who find themselves in situations that are not right for them." She was the first woman (1977) to become a judge on Massachusetts' Supreme Judicial Court. Before that she was an assistant district attorney, division chief in the Massachusetts attorney general's office and superior court judge.

Lila Fenwick (Harvard Law 1956) was quoted as saying: "I knew I was going to be a lawyer when I was a little girl … It never occurred to me that there were going to be any obstacles." But there were obstacles: Many of them. And she faced them without doubting "that she would achieve professional success, despite the racism she grew up with and the sexism she encountered in school and beyond."

Justice Ruth Bader Ginsburg (Harvard Law 1956–1958, Columbia 1959): Powerful independent voice, appeals court judge [U.S. Court of Appeals in the D.C. Circuit], practicing attorney and law professor who established a reputation as an advocate for women's causes and accomplished a stack of "firsts", argued six cases on sex discrimination before the U.S. Supreme Court before joining the Court. She is the second woman in U.S. history to sit on the highest court in the United States of America.

Judge Gladys Kessler (Harvard Law 1962): Part "of the first wave of women to attain seats on the bench." Landmark cases for which she has issued rulings include the government suit recovering damages from tobacco companies and the order requiring the U.S. Justice Department to release names of people detained by the government after the September 11, 2001, attacks on the U.S. Pentagon and World Trade Center. She has been associate judge of the Superior Court of the District of Columbia and currently sits on the U.S. District Court for the District of Columbia. Quoted in an interview, Judge Kessler said, "Women have a responsibility to make a difference in the legal system and the administration of justice."

Janet Reno (Harvard Law 1963): First woman U.S. Attorney General. Before going to Washington, she had been state attorney for Dade County, Florida. She "instituted drug courts ... and focused on providing education and health care for children." Running in a Florida gubernatorial race, she observed, "If people won't run for political office because they think it's beneath them, then democracy is at risk in this world."

Judge Judith Rogers (Harvard Law 1964): In a February 2007 case centered around a Bush administration anti-terrorism law prohibiting U.S.-held detainees at Guantanamo Bay, Cuba, from challenging their detention before federal judges, Judge Rogers dissented. She wrote that the law was "inconsistent with the Constitution's clause limiting the suspension of habeas corpus, a long-standing principle of U.S. law." Judge Rogers was associate judge then chief judge for the D.C. Court of Appeals before taking her current position on the U.S. Court of Appeals for the D.C. Circuit.

Former U.S. Representative Patricia (Pat) Schroeder (Harvard Law 1964) was a twelve-term Colorado Member of the United States House of Representatives and one-time (1986) candidate for the office of U.S. President. She was known for her stands on human rights, women's issues, family issues, and ethical standards in public office. In her memoir *24 Years of House Work ... and the Place Is Still a Mess*, she wrote: "The years of hard work and struggle have led to some triumphs ... but we also have to think about how far we have not come, and how much is left to do to improve the health, status and well-being of American women."

Former Congresswoman Elizabeth Holtzman (Harvard 1965) was the "youngest woman ever elected to the U. S. Congress." In the President Richard M. Nixon Watergate years she was a leading critic on the U.S. House Judiciary Committee. She was also a member of a presidential committee on Nazi war criminals and worked "to declassify the U.S. government's war crimes files."

Senator Elizabeth Dole (Harvard 1965): the first woman elected U.S. Senator from North Carolina, one-time candidate for the office of U.S. President. Her executive branch offices have included membership on the Federal Trade Commission, first woman Secretary of the U.S. Department of Transportation, and Secretary of the U.S. Department of Labor.

V

U.S. Women Policymakers, Lawmakers, Peacemakers

Past to Present (Barbara Jordan, National Unity)

Round and round they go. Government voices mass media ordain "authorities" and repeatedly put before the public are essentially *one* voice: corporate media/government: a voice that is unbearably banal, shallow, made to misinform. This does not mean however that government has been without truer voices: original, deeply thoughtful voices on critical issues of our time. In the post-Cold War era (in 2007 some began calling it the new Cold War era) as Washington has waged war against one after another foreign nation and against the American people's Constitution—to form a more perfect union (not an imperial presidency), to establish justice, insure domestic tranquility (peace among all our diversities), to provide for the common defense (not attack other countries), to promote the general welfare (social, environmental, economic, physical well being), and to secure liberty (living democracy) for our future—some accomplished women in the U.S. Congress have tried to stem the war tide. Often they have taken their lead from the words and work of women in past congresses.

"We are a people in a quandary about the present," declared a history-making lawmaker in a historic speech. "We are a people in search of our future," said U.S. Congresswoman Barbara Jordan on the near eve (July 12, 1976) of a new presidency. Thirty years on America feels dangerously fractured and in need of National Unity, a sense of Shared Destiny for the Common Good. This 1956 magna cum laude graduate of Texas Southern University, 1959 Jurist Doctor of Boston University continues:

We are a people in search of a national community. We are a people trying not only to solve the problems of the present: unemployment, inflation … but we are attempting on a larger scale to fulfill the promise of America. We are attempting to fulfill our national purpose; to create and sustain a society in which all of us are equal …

We believe that the people are the source of all governmental power; that the authority of the people is to be extended, not restricted …

This can be accomplished only by providing each citizen with every opportunity to participate in the management of the government. They must have that, we believe. We believe that the government which represents the authority of all the people, not just one interest group, but all the people, has an obligation to actively—underscore actively—seek to remove those obstacles which would block individual achievement … The government must remove them, seek to remove them …

Let us heed the voice of the people and recognize their common sense. If we do not, we not only blaspheme our political heritage, we ignore the common ties that bind all Americans. Many fear the future. Many are distrustful of their leaders, and believe that their voices are never heard. Many seek only to satisfy their private wants; to satisfy private interests. But this is the great danger America faces. That we will cease to be one nation and become instead a collection of interest groups: city against suburb, region against region, individual against individual. Each seeking to satisfy private wants. If that happens, who then will speak for America? Who then will speak for the common good? …

A nation is formed by the willingness of each of us to share in the responsibility for upholding the common good. A government is invigorated when each of us is willing to participate in shaping the future of this nation … Let each person do his or her part. If one citizen is unwilling to participate, all of us are going to suffer.

For the American idea, though it is shared by all of us, is realized in each one of us ...

We as public servants must set an example for the rest of the nation. It is hypocritical for the public official to admonish and exhort the people to uphold the common good if we are derelict in upholding the common good. More is required. More is required of public officials than slogans and handshakes and press releases. More is required. We must hold ourselves strictly accountable. We must provide the people with a vision of the future.

If we promise as public officials, we must deliver. If we as public officials propose, we must produce. If we say to the American people, 'It is time for you to be sacrificial'—sacrifice. If the public official says that, we [public officials] must be the first to give. We must be. And again, if we make mistakes, we must be willing to admit them. We have to do that. What we have to do is strike a balance between the idea that government should do everything and the idea, the belief that government ought to do nothing. Strike a balance.

Let there be no illusions about the difficulty of forming this kind of a national community. It's tough, difficult, not easy. But a spirit of harmony will survive in America only if each of us remembers that we share a common destiny; if each of us remembers, when self-interest and bitterness seem to prevail, that we share a common destiny.

I have confidence that we can form this kind of national unity ...

Women's voices must be heard. Their difference is essential and must be present at the table, in the debate. Their leadership must be unrestricted in all branches of U.S. government: legislative, executive and judicial. In 2007 the world had eight female Presidents: in Chile, Finland, Ireland, Israel (Acting), Latvia, Liberia, The Philippines, and Switzerland. The world had five prime ministers: in Germany, Jamaica, New Zealand, Mozambique, and The Netherlands Antilles. For the first six months of 2007 German Chancellor Angela Merkel was arguably the most influential person in the world. In addition to being Germany's head of state, she led the European Union as Germany held the six-month presidency of the twenty-seven nation bloc, and she hosted the Group of Eight (Britain, France, Germany, Italy, Russia, the United States of America, Canada, Japan) "Plus Five" (Brazil, China, India, Mexico, and South Africa) Summit at Heiligendamm, Germany. U.S. voters, a majority of whom are women, have never elected a woman President of the United States of America.

The Center for American Women and Politics at Rutgers University in New Jersey reported after the 2006 elections that in the United States eighty-seven women had been elected to the U. S. House of Representatives and Senate. Women took sixteen of the one hundred Senate seats and seventy-one (plus three Delegates) of the four hundred and thirty-five House seats. The following data excerpted by permission of the Center illustrates that though U.S. voters have never elected a woman to the office of President of the United States the country possesses a substantial pool of highly qualified and accomplished women who are eligible to hold the highest government elective executive office.

Eligible 2007 for U. S. Presidency

U. S. Senate 16

AK U.S. Sen. Lisa Murkowski	MN U.S. Sen. Amy Klobuchar
AR U.S. Sen. Blanche Lincoln	MO U.S. Sen. Claire McCaskill
CA U.S. Sen. Barbara Boxer	NC U.S. Sen. Elizabeth Dole
CA U.S. Sen. Dianne Feinstein	NY U.S. Sen. Hillary Rodham Clinton
LA U.S. Sen. Mary Landrieu	TX U.S. Sen. Kay Bailey Hutchison
ME U.S. Sen. Susan Collins	
ME U.S. Sen. Olympia Snowe	WA U.S. Sen. Patty Murray
MD U.S. Sen. Barbara Mikulski	WA U.S. Sen. Maria Cantwell
MI U.S. Sen. Debbie Stabenow	

U.S. **House** of Representatives 71, plus 3 Delegates

AZ U.S. Rep. 008 Gabrielle Giffords

CA U.S. Rep. 005 Doris Matsui
006 Lynn Woolsey
008 Nancy Pelosi
009 Barbara Lee
010 Ellen Tauscher
014 Anna Eshoo
016 Zoe Lofgren
023 Lois Capps
032 Hilda Solis
033 Diane Watson
034 Lucille Roybal-Allard
035 Maxine Waters
036 Jane Harman
037 Juanita Millender-McDonald
[note: d. 4/7/2007]
038 Grace Napolitano
039 Linda Sanchez
045 Mary Bono
047 Loretta Sanchez
053 Susan Davis

CO U.S. Rep. 001 Diana DeGette
U.S. Rep. 004 Marilyn Musgrave

CT U.S. Rep. 003 Rosa DeLauro

DC U.S. Del. Eleanor Holmes Norton

FL U.S. Rep. 003 Corinne Brown
005 Ginny Brown-Waite
011 Kathy Castor
018 Ileana Ros-Lehtinen
020 Debbie Wasserman Schultz

GU U.S. Del. Madeleine Bordallo

HI U.S. Rep. 002 Mazie Hirono

IL U.S. Rep. 008 Melissa Bean
009 Jan Schakowsky
013 Judy Biggert

IN U.S. Rep. 007 Julia Carson

KS U.S. Rep. 002 Nancy Boyda

MI U.S. Rep. 010 Candice Miller
013 Carolyn Cheeks Kilpatrick

MN U.S. Rep. 004 Betty McCollum
U.S. Rep. 006 Michele Bachmann

MO U.S. Rep. 008 Jo Ann Emerson

NC U.S. Rep. 005 Virginia Foxx

	009 Sue Myrick
NH U.S. Rep.	001 Carol Shea-Porter
NM U.S. Rep.	001 Heather Wilson
NV U.S. Rep.	001 Shelley Berkley
NY U.S. Rep.	004 Carolyn McCarthy
	011 Yvette Clarke
	012 Nydia Velazquez
	014 Carolyn Maloney
	018 Nita Lowey
	020 Kirsten Gillibrand
	028 Louise Slaughter
OH U.S. Rep.	002 Jean Schmidt
	009 Marcia "Marcy" Kaptur
	011 Stephanie Tubbs Jones
	013 Betty Sutton
	015 Deborah Pryce
OK U.S. Rep.	005 Mary Fallin
OR U.S. Rep.	005 Darlene Hooley
PA U.S. Rep.	013 Allyson Schwartz
SD U.S. Rep.	at large Stephanie Herseth [Sandlin]
TN U.S. Rep.	007 Marsha Blackburn
TX U.S. Rep.	012 Kay Granger
	018 Sheila Jackson Lee
	030 Eddie Bernice Johnson
VA U.S. Rep.	001 Jo Ann Davis
	002 Thelma Drake
VI U.S. Del.	Donna Christensen
WA U.S. Rep.	005 Cathy McMorris
WI U.S. Rep.	002 Tammy Baldwin
	004 Gwendolynne "Gwen" Moore
WV U.S. Rep.	002 Shelley Moore Capito
WY U.S. Rep.	Barbara L. Cubin

Source: Center for American Women and Politics, Eagleton Institute of Politics, Rutgers, The State University of New Jersey, 191 Ryders Lane, New Brunswick, NJ 08901-8557, (732) 932-9384—Fax: (732) 932-0014

The Center for American Women and Politics also reported in 2007 that women held nine state governorships and sixty-seven other statewide elective executive offices. State legislatures in the United States seated 1,734 women.

Governors—9

AK	Sarah Palin
AZ	Janet Napolitano
CT	M. Jodi Rell
DE	Ruth Ann Minner
HI	Linda Lingle
KS	Kathleen Sebelius
LA	Kathleen Blanco
MI	Jennifer Granholm
WA	Christine Gregoire

Lieutenant Governors—11

CO	Barbara O'Brien
IA	Patty Judge
IN	Becky Skillman
MN	Carol Molnau
MS	Amy Tuck
NC	Beverly Perdue *
NM	Diane D. Denish
OK	Jari Askins*
PA	Catherine Baker Knoll
RI	Elizabeth Roberts *
WI	Barbara Lawton

* Elected independent of the governor.

Attorney General—4

IL	Lisa Madigan
MA	Martha Coakley
MN	Lori Swanson
NV	Catherine Cortez Masto

Secretary of **State—12**

AL	Beth Chapman
AZ	Jan Brewer
CA	Debra Bowen
CT	Susan Bysiewicz
GA	Karen Handel
MI	Terri Lynn Land
MO	Robin Carnahan
NC	Elaine Marshall
NM	Mary Herrera
OH	Jennifer Brunner
VT	Deborah Markowitz
WV	Betty Ireland

State **Treasurer/chief** Financial Officer—10

AL	Kay Ivey
AR	Martha Shoffner
CO	Cary Kennedy
CT	Denise Nappier
FL	Alex Sink
KS	Lynn Jenkins
MO	Sarah Steelman
ND	Kelly Schmidt
NV	Kate Marshall
WI	Dawn Marie Sass

State **Auditor**—6

AL	Samantha Shaw
KY	Crit Luallen
MN	Rebecca Otto
MO	Susan Montee
OH	Mary Taylor
WY	Rita Meyer

State **Comptroller/controller** 4

CT	Nancy Wyman
ID	Donna M. Jones
NV	Kim Wallin
TX	Susan Combs

Chief State **Education** Official 8 (title varies from state to state)

GA	Kathy Cox
IN	Suellen K. Reed
MT	Linda McCulloch
NC	June Atkinson
OK	Sandy Garrett
OR	Susan Castillo
WA	Teresa Bergeson
WI	Elizabeth Burmaster

Commissioners

Commissioner of Insurance—2

KS	Sandy Praeger
OK	Kim Holland

Commissioner of Labor—1

NC	Cherie Killian Berry

Corporation Commissioner—2

AZ	Kristin K. Mayes
OK	Denise Bode

Public Service Commissioner—5

AL	Jan Cook
AL	Susan D. Parker

GA   Angela Speir

ND   Susan E. Wefald

NE   Anne Boyle

Public Regulation Commissioner—1

NM   Carol K. Sloan

Railroad Commissioner—1

TX   Elizabeth Ames Jones

Source: Center for American Women and Politics, Eagleton Institute of Politics, Rutgers, The State University of New Jersey, 191 Ryders Lane, New Brunswick, NJ 08901-8557, (732) 932-9384—Fax: (732) 932-0014.

California Rep. **Juanita Millender-McDonald** (1938-2007) http://bioguide.congress.gov/.

Mississippi Freedom Democratic Party founder **Fannie Lou Hamer** (1917-1977). Photograph by Warren K. Leffler, 1964 Aug. 22. Location of Original: U.S. News and World Report Collection: LC-U9-12470-B

Texas Rep. **Barbara Jordan** (1936-1996). Photograph by Tom O'Halloran. Location of Original: U.S. News and World Report Collection: Library of Congress-U9-32512.

New York Rep. **Shirley Chisholm** (1924-2005). Photograph by Tom O O'Halloran. Location of Original: U.S. News and World Report Collection: Library of Congress-U9-25383.

In Memoriam

California Rep. **Barbara Lee.**
www.hsph.harvard.edu/.

California Rep. **Lynn Woolsey.**
http://bioguide.congress.gov/.

California Rep. **Anna Eshoo.**
http://bioguide.congress.gov/.

California Rep. (Speaker of the
House) **Nancy Pelosi**
http://bioguide.congress.gov/.

Former Colorado Rep. **Patricia Schroeder.**
http://bioguide.congress.gov/.
Author of 24 Years of HouseWork... and the
Place is Still a Mess: My Life in Politics.

Former Oregon Rep. **Elizabeth Furse.**
Peace advocate, born in
Nairobi, Kenya.
http://bioguide.congress.gov/.

Former Illinois Sen. **Carol Moseley Braun.**
http://biouide.congress.gov/.

Former New York Rep., vice presidential
candidate **Geraldine Ferraro**.
http://bioguide.congress.gov/.

Maine Senator **Susan Collins**
http://collins.senate.gov/.

New York Rep. **Nydia Velazquez**
http://bioguide.congress.gov/.

Oregon Rep. **Darlene Hooley**
http://bioguide.congress.gov/.

North Carolina Sen. **Elizabeth Dole**
speaks at MADD news conference
Also cited at http://dole.senate.gov/.

Texas Rep. **Sheila Jackson Lee** questioning new NASA administrator.
Photo Courtesy of David Sims June 28 , 2005.
http://www.jacksonlee.house.gov/.

California Rep. **Maxine Waters**
http://bioguide.congress.gov/.

New York Rep. **Carolyn McCarthy**
http://bioguide.congress.gov/

Texas Sen. **Kay Bailey Hutchison**,
commencement speaker, Austin
State University.
http://hutchison.senate.gov/.

Minnesota Rep. **Betty McCollum**
http://bioguide.congress.gov/.

Connecticut Rep. **Rosa DeLauro**
http://bioguide.congress.gov/.

California Rep. **Linda Sanchez**
http://bioguide.congress.gov/.

Indiana Rep. **Julia Carson**
http://bioguide.congress.gov/.

Ohio Rep. **Marcia (Marcy) Kaptur**
http://bioguide.congress.gov/.

"Money shouts its priorities. The rest of us are put on hold, growing more disenchanted by the minute ... Government has become a machine that runs only when gold coins are inserted."

Hon. Patricia Schroeder (b. 1940)
Twelve-term Member of the United States House of Representatives
(1972–1996)

Eligible But Can They Afford the Admission Price?

S
even years into the twenty-first century seems like the Dark Ages for ordinary women aspiring to campaign viably for and win a seat in high public office. Because the average woman is incapable of claiming access to obscene millions needed to launch and sustain primary and general election campaigns, this woman—and there are many of them—might as well be living in the Dark Ages.

The Center for Responsive Politics (its Open Secrets website) reported in 2007 that the cost of winning an average seat in the U.S. House of Representatives in 1992 was approximately $543,000; for a U.S. Senate seat the cost was $3.9 million. New York Senator Alfonse D'Amato that year had spent $9.2 million to defeat his opponent; his opponent spent $6.4 million. California millionaire Michael Huffington spent $5.4 million for a U.S. House seat to unseat Gloria Ochoa; she spent $663,027. Millionaire Jon Corzine in 2000 spent a record-setting $63.2 million on his race for the Senate, $60 million of which "came from his own pocket." In 2006 the New York campaign for U.S. Senate cost $40,828.991, up from $27,159,681 in 1998. In 2004 the campaign expenditure total for U.S. House, Democrats and Republicans, excluding actual amount raised, was $450,169,750; for the U.S. Senate the total was $243,890,824. Average spending in 2004 for U.S. House campaigns, Democrats and Republicans (435 candidates), totaled $1,034.873; for U.S. Senate campaigns, Democrats and Republicans (34 candidates), 7,173,260. In 2004 the total price of presidential and congressional elections, according to the Center for Responsive Politics, was at least $4 billion. In 2000 the price was nearly $3 billion, in 1996 it was $2.2 billion, and in 1992 the price was 1.8 billion.

When there is potential—and there is *always* potential—or actual competition, the exorbitant admission price drives out competition, rendering the U.S. system undemocratic. Driving up costs are expensive broadcast advertisements, political consultants, along with day-to-day management and public relations overhead and staffing. Money, incumbency, and non competitiveness keep women (the majority population) from waging viable campaigns and being elected to high public office. In her book *24 Years of House Work … and the Place is Still a Mess: My Life in Politics,* former Congresswoman Patricia Schroeder laid out what women and voters are up against. People "hold their noses and turn their backs on the whole system, which virtually ensures that fat cats and their vested interests will triumph and that the price of admission to the political career is too high for all but the grandees of society or those who owe their professional lives to them," she wrote. "Money does too much talking in Washington. Every senator, every representative, even the president awakens each morning with a number in his head that will drive the whole day. The number is the amount of money that must be raised that day for his reelection. If he fails, the next day's number will be even higher."

Four years after publication of Schroeder's book the Shays-Meehan campaign finance reform legislation made its way to the floor of the House of Representatives. Some of the women in Congress, such as Representative Anna Eshoo, thought it was a milestone. Eschoo said "by banning the obscene sums of 'soft money' that pour into the coffers of both political parties, Shays-Meehan will help restore the public's confidence in our government and our country." Mass media ignored the significance of this legislation but sixteen Congresswomen had voted for the 2002 phase of campaign finance reform legislation and several of these women—California Congresswomen Anna Eshoo, Jane Harman, Lois Capps, Susan Davis, Lynn Woolsey and Nancy Pelosi, Oregon's Darlene Hooley, Michigan's Lynn Rivers, Minnesota's Betty McCollum, Indiana's Julia Carson, Ohio's Marcy Kaptur, New York's Carolyn McCarthy, Nydia Velazquez and Louise Slaughter, and Connecticut's Rosa DeLauro and Nancy Johnson—praised the effort on their Congressional Web sites.

But campaign finance remains unreformed. Corporations, whose money has been granted First Amendment rights over people's democratic rights, decide who contends for public office, who gets air time, and who gets elected and reelected to public office. Disheartening for the U.S. electorate is the belief that political office is being bought and sold for private interests: quid pro quos, winks-and-nods promising kickbacks on all sides.

The words and work of Shirley Chisholm in the 1960s and 1970s, Barbara Jordan and Geraldine Ferraro in the 1970s and 1980s, the Year of the Woman in the 1990s gave women every reason to believe, not only that America was rich with politically astute, accomplished women; but that soon Americans would elect their first progressive woman head of state. It did not happen. The country's failure to take women's legislative leadership sufficiently seriously and to elect a woman to the highest elective office means that women's liberation in America is incomplete. Moreover women will not win in numbers commensurate with their population numbers until the United States ensures clean, open and democratic election systems. And clean elections will not happen until Americans elect sufficient numbers of independent, "unbossed and unbought," progressive women lawmakers committed to electoral reform: women who will introduce, vote for, and guide into law loophole-proof, clean, democratically open (uniform, publicly financed, federally regulated) and ethically executed elections-related practices.

"I've always felt that the most valuable asset you have in politics is your word. When you can't be trusted to tell the truth, you can't be entrusted with the country's future ..."

Hon. Patricia Schroeder (b. 1940)
Twelve-term Member of the United States House of Representatives
(1972–1996)

VI

U.S. Women Credentialed but Off Center Stage

Kathleen Sebelius in Kansas

Kansas Governor Kathleen Sebelius was giving her State of the State speech at the start of 2007. She was thinking about strength in unity, cooperation, and state and national initiatives to lead the world (as Chancellor Merkel has led from her country) in the care of the environment for ourselves and our posterity. On cooperation and economic empowerment, she said: "There is no reason for the future of rural Kansas to be one of faded signs and empty storefronts. The challenges faced by these communities require cooperation between families, businesses, government and organizations that focus on rural areas ..." On energy conservation and the future, she continued, "The question of where we get our energy is ... no longer just an economic issue, nor solely an issue of national security. Quite simply, we have a moral obligation to be good stewards of this state, because we are only here for a short time and we will ultimately pass it on to our children ... There's no reason our state should not lead the nation in wind energy. That's why I've included money in my budget to plan for transmission lines to move electricity from wind farms to customers. But our responsibility as stewards also requires us to protect our natural treasures like the Heart of the Flint Hills from development, as we will ... We must call on Congress to commit to funding additional research and development efforts to accelerate our energy security, and to adopt strict national emission standards for our environment ... I believe state government should be a conservation leader and vigorously seek to eliminate energy waste, as we have done with spending waste ..."

Shirley Chisholm [b. 1924–d. 2005]
"Candidate of the people"

> I am not the candidate of black America, although I am black and proud, said another pioneering lawmaker. "I am not the candidate of the women's movement in this country, although I am a woman, and I am equally proud of that. I am not the candidate of any political bosses or special interests … I am the candidate of the people.

New York Congresswoman Shirley Anita St. Hill Chisholm lived eight decades and left American politics and politicians a lasting legacy in her words and work. Shirley Chisholm was different. She personified noble independence—the quality of ethical behavior, new blood and fresh ideas she called for throughout her political life. U. S. Representative Chisholm ran for the Democratic nomination for U.S. president in 1972. Logging her experiences in her book *The Good Fight*, Chisholm warned the Democratic party that its viability would depend on bringing in new blood, drawing in women and minorities and treating them with the respect of equals. She urged the party to practice coalition building and to challenge the status quo. Seeing little difference between "liberal" and "conservative" parties— "One talks a better game," she once said—Chisholm urged the kind of change in people and political parties that embraces and respects diversity.

She billed herself a politician who was "unbossed and unbought." Despite enormous odds in 1972 she entered the race and campaigned all across America for the office of U.S. President. At the time, she was less than two terms into what would become seven terms in the U.S. House of Representatives. The press wanted to know why she was running for the highest office in the land. She said she was running "to demonstrate sheer will and refusal to accept the status quo." The critics said she was running for symbolism; for leverage at that year's Democratic National Convention; for ego gratification. She shot back: "It takes a good opinion of one's abilities to seriously offer oneself as a candidate for the hardest job in the world, … but there are more satisfying ways of expressing one's self-esteem than going on a killing nine-month schedule of campaigning and going hundreds of thousands of dollars in debt."

Jeannette Rankin was the first woman elected to the U.S. House of Representatives. She stood against the first and second world wars, and against the Vietnam War, as did Chisholm. At the age of ninety-two Rankin pondered running again for public office. She too was asked why she was running. Her answer seemed to echo in Chisholm's stand against the status quo. Rankin's answer: "Just to have someone to vote for."

Like Hubert Humphrey, Scoop Jackson and George McGovern—who were also running the year America was in another crisis—Shirley Chisholm "was running for the office of president to win." The year she ran the United States was mired in Vietnam. The Nixon administration, blinded by zeal to grab a second term in office, had burgled the Democratic Headquarters located at a hotel and office complex called the Watergate. The co-conspirators had attempted to cover up their crimes and ended up supplying probable cause for presidential impeachment. Chisholm's history-making year was the year the Senate-passed Equal Rights Amendment (ERA) went to the states for ratification. It was the year the U.S. Supreme court ruled the death penalty unconstitutional and busing an acceptable means toward school integration. America's Union was divided against itself. And Congresswoman Shirley Chisholm was tired of old-line liberal and conservative politicians; tired of tokenism and "orders-taking" and "errand-running." She believed the Democratic Party, indeed the whole political system in America, needed new blood and uncorrupt systems. She wanted to see ethical politicians serving in a fair, open and uncorrupt system. Thirty years ago Chisholm was promoting what today is still worth pushing for and achieving. She believed campaigns should be financed entirely by public funds. Regulations should be tightened and enforced. Political campaigns should be shortened.

"Everywhere in this country," she said, "there are men and women who have real ability and new solutions to offer, but they will never have a chance to serve in public office because they do not have the money to run and win. Meanwhile, candidates who are wealthy to start with, or who are not scrupulous about where they get their financial support, run well-financed campaigns that land them in office—where they become, with few exceptions, exactly the men and women whom we ought not to have representing us."

America's 2004 campaign and election processes were seriously flawed resulting in seriously flawed elected and re-elected officials. Chisholm was right in 1972. Her words and work are still right. The system is discriminatory, undemocratic, and antithetical to any form of democracy at any level of society. It's not good enough to quip that everybody else's system is so much worse that ours is, by default, the best in the world. "Are all wisdom, all talent, all leadership, all intelligence, all ability, all creativity concentrated in … one group?" Chisholm asks. "If not—as is obvious they are not—is not our society losing a great deal by its habitual pattern of delegating power: a few white men lead, everyone else follows? Could it be that the persistence of poverty, hunger, racism, war, semi-literacy and unemployment is partly due to the fact that we have excluded so many persons from the processes that make and carry out social policies?"

Chisholm said "We must turn away from the control of the prosaic [the unimaginative, the dull and commonplace], the privileged, and the old-line, tired politicians to open our society to the energies and abilities of countless new groups of Americans—women, blacks, browns, Indians, Orientals and youth—so that they can develop their own full potential, and thereby participate equally and enthusiastically in building a strong and just society, rich in its diversity and noble in its quality of life."

A party does not make serious change—or convince people that it is serious about making change—by eleventh-hour voter registration drives and free rides to the polls. When a party is serious about change it cultivates relations with diversity over the long term. "Working together means getting out of the nine-to-five, draw-your-pay, drink-some-beer-and-watch-television routine," Chisholm wrote. "It means becoming more aware of the world and society we live in and the people in it, developing deeper, more meaningful interrelations and, through them, coming to understand the purpose of our own existence … Just as men will be freed when women are liberated, blacks and whites will emerge as more vital and ennobled beings when they can meet each other face to face as man and woman of equal worth and potential": A politics of equality.

What Chisholm called coalition politics, requires a non-hierarchical structure. "It is much easier to set the organization up in hierarchies, with the leader, his lieutenants, their sergeants, and the rank and file at the bottom," she said. "But a democratic political movement is not an army; it exists only for the sake of the ordinary people who make up its body, and the most important consideration is to organize it so it responds to their needs and seeks to fulfill them."

When Shirley Chisholm set out that January day to run for the presidency of the United States, she said of herself: "I am not the candidate of black America, although I am black and proud. I am not the candidate of the women's movement in this country, although I am a woman, and I am equally proud of that. I am not the candidate of any political bosses or special interests ... I am the candidate of the people."

Chisholm's values, her courage, her work ethic, her *good* fight served our country well. Adopting her values would go a long way toward improving politics, politicians and leadership in America. We Americans "are a dynamic people," she said, "because of our rugged individuality and our cherished diversity, because of our belief in human dignity, because of our generosity and goodwill to our fellow men, and most importantly, because of our tradition of moving forward to actively confront those problems which plague us in a world growing more complex each year."

Shirley Chisholm began and ended her career as an educator. For a generation in the seventies and eighties she was among America's best politicians. From 1964 to1968 she was a member of the New York State legislature. From 1968 to 1983, she was member of the U.S. House of Representatives. In 1972 she ran for the U.S. Office of President. Reflecting on American progress and her work within that context, she said: "That I am a national figure because I was the first person in 192 years to be at once a [Member of Congress], black and a woman proves, I think, that our society is not yet either just or free."

Woolsey and Lee
Peace and Justice Duo in Congress

By the summer of 2005 the Bush administration's U.S.A. Patriot Act was already infringing civil liberties. It was headed toward re-authorization. California Congresswoman Lynn Woolsey spoke in opposition on the floor of the House of Representatives: "Just as a bad movie is often followed by an even worse sequel, so it is with the PATRIOT Act ... Basic civil liberties continue to be in jeopardy; the bill expands police powers; it continues to authorize invasive violations of our medical records, our library borrowing habits, and other private affairs that have nothing to do with terrorism ... [In] defense of freedom, we are undermining freedom ... Patriotism means affirming and celebrating the values that have made America strong for more than two centuries. Legislation that violates several constitutional amendments has no business calling itself the PATRIOT Act."

The turn of the new millennium saw another Congresswoman emerging in the spirit of Jeannette Rankin. Congresswoman Barbara Lee distinguished herself in the dark fall days of 2001 by standing alone against war, against more terrorism. In dissenting on a joint resolution (H. J. Res. 64) that ceded future congressional authority to the U.S. President to use military force in response to "terrorist" attacks, she said: "Our deepest fears now haunt us. September 11 changed the world. Yet I am convinced that military action will not prevent further acts of international terrorism against the United States."

Old wisdom says war makes more war, violence more violence. Disrespect coupled with arms distribution turns on us: Turns against us. If we are truly changed by the events of September 11, 2001, as many insist, then let us be changed through-and-through: Changed to act anew; To act lawfully, non-violently. In Barbara Lee's patriotism are constitutional principles insuring domestic tranquility, providing for the common defense, promoting the general welfare, securing the blessings of liberty to ourselves and those who come after us. Lee is America's kind of patriot: one whose love of country wants to protect and preserve it, its principles and its people.

Congresswoman Lee's record in state and federal legislatures shows her love of America. She has worked for health, education and welfare; for affordable housing and economic development. She has sponsored and co-sponsored legislation to eradicate HIV/AIDS in California and throughout the United States and Africa, preferring grants over loans to assist poor people and countries in the global fight against the disease. She has worked for schools and school children and youth, and college graduates with student loans. Credentialed in social work education, the congresswoman has worked on behalf of women generally, and particularly on behalf of black men in California. She has publicly recognized women's achievements including the work of former U.S. Congresswoman and presidential candidate Shirley Chisholm.

Congresswoman Lee has established a record of social- and human-centered legislation. The day after that dark September morning she voted for H. J. Res. 61 condemning the terrorist attacks, extending condolences to victims and their families, commending rescue workers, supporting President Bush in "punishing the perpetrators of the attacks," and decreeing September 12th a national day of unity and mourning. She voted for H. Con. Res. 225 to express the sense of the U.S. Congress that Americans fly the American flag. She voted for H.R. 2882 to speed payments of benefits to families of public safety officers killed or injured in the September 11th attacks. She voted for H.R. 2884 to provide tax relief to the victims of the attacks. She voted for H.R. 2888 to provide $40 billion in emergency funding for increased public safety, anti-terrorism activities, disaster recovery efforts, and assistance for the victims of the tragedy.

In her dissent against mob-think fomenting a "lynching," Barbara Lee personified the best of America. The President can wage a war even without this resolution (H.J. Res. 64), the congresswoman said. But "some of us must urge the use of restraint. Our country is in a state of mourning. Some of us must say, let's step back for a moment and think through the implications of our action today so that it does not spiral out of control." Quoting a member of the clergy that day, she concluded: "As we act, let us not become the evil that we deplore."

When the *irrationalists* rejected her advice she co-sponsored legislation opposing what she saw coming. This new legislation condemned "bigotry, racism and violence against Arab Americans, American Muslims, and Americans from South Asia following the terrorist attacks."

In the summer of 2005 U.S. Representative Barbara Lee introduced H. Con. Res. 197, a resolution co-sponsored by eighty-six members of the House of Representatives, opposing U.S. permanent military bases in Iraq. The legislation declared "that it is the policy of the United States not to enter into any base agreement with the Government of Iraq that would lead to a permanent United States military presence in Iraq."

In the spring of 2006 Lee introduced legislation with twenty-five co-sponsors asking the U.S. President to submit to the Congress his plans concerning Iran. House Resolution 846 requested the President and directed the Secretary of State: "to provide to the House of Representatives certain documents in their possession relating to strategies and plans either designed to cause regime change in or for the use of military force against Iran."

Congresswoman Lee's five-year legislative crusade received no national media attention. But America's liberal progressives were loudly pleased as punch when men in Congress appeared finally to find their backbones, even if, as one writer put it, they were taking orders from military generals. In late November 2005 media-made high profiled male members of the U.S. House of Representatives said to the president it's time to bring America's men and women home from this abominably illegal, immoral Cheney-Halliburton-Rumsfeld-Rice-Bush war. It's time to save our troops by setting a strategy, a timetable and; by god, bringing them home.

Asia *Times* reported at the time that Pennsylvania Representative John Murtha, one of the media's chosen "has historically been so close to the military that many political observers will conclude that he is speaking for senior officers who have grown increasingly convinced that the war has been a major strategic mistake." Murtha may or may not have been taking orders from generals. But one woman Member of Congress clearly was not.

California Congresswoman Lynn Woolsey, like Congresswoman Lee, had long led the campaign on Capitol Hill and in her home district to bring the troops home, salvage U.S. credibility in the world, and bind up the wounds of a country devastated by Bush's wars. Representative Woolsey was the first member of Congress to call for the troops to come home from Iraq. By sponsoring House Congressional Resolution 35 in January 2005, Congresswoman Woolsey began a public movement hoped to start an avalanche. The resolution co-sponsored by 34 House Members recognized mounting disasters in what was then a two-year-old war against Iraq. Disasters already evident included the administration's pretext for war; budget overruns and waste; mounting U.S. military dead (by mid-year 2007 known U.S. troop deaths were approaching 4,000) and wounded in the tens of thousands, untold hundreds of thousands of Iraqi men, women and children dead; and a foreign policy that was (and is) provoking insurgencies ricocheting violence across the Middle East. The January 2005 resolution did not call for a "cut-and-run" policy as the Bush administration alleged and continued to maintain. It called instead for creating and carrying out a plan to begin the immediate withdrawal of United States Armed Forces from Iraq; producing a plan for reconstructing Iraq's civil and economic infrastructure; convening an emergency meeting of Iraq's leadership and its neighbors, the United Nations, and the Arab League to create an international peacekeeping force in Iraq to replace United States Armed Forces with Iraqi police and Iraqi National Guard forces to ensure Iraq's security; and taking steps to provide the Iraqi people with the opportunity to completely control their internal affairs.

The Bush White House, the corporate mass media, and most of Congress (each feeding the other) ignored Congresswoman Woolsey's resolution. But she did not stop her crusade for America and for all those people dying and displaced in Iraq. In the fall of 2005 she tried again: this time convening a hearing to obtain expert testimony on how best to get out of Iraq. The time had come, she said, to "fill the policy vacuum and break the silence on Capitol Hill." As outrages mounted against Bush's war, the tide began turning. Anti-war activists moved from fringe to mainstream. Woolsey recognized this as she convened hearings in September. She recited for the record a long train of delusions and abuses:

> Some of us have dissented from the very beginning, based on the belief that the doctrine of pre-emptive war is inhuman and

immoral. Others were shocked that the Administration's ratio-
nale for war turned out to be based on dubious intelligence at
best and outright lies at worst. Others became disillusioned by
the Abu Ghraib outrage, or the failure to outfit our soldiers with
proper body and vehicle armor. Still others jumped off the [pro-
war] bandwagon when it became clear that the Administration
was deluding itself into believing that there would be no insur-
gency, that we'd be greeted as liberators, that this mission would
require only minimal manpower and a few billion dollars. And
for some, the last straw has been the blinding incompetence of
the war effort: the failure to prevent looting; the failure to secure
munitions sites; the dissolving of the Iraqi army; the lack of an
effective plan to secure the peace after the end of major combat
operations ...

Mary Ann Wright and Cindy Sheehan
Camp Casey, Antiwar

On one occasion Woolsey suggested that the pressure needed to get a change
in U.S. policy and U.S. troops out of Iraq required more than street protests. But protests were important. And women led critical demonstrations
against war and occupation. In their protests many women made great sacrifices. On the eve of President George W. Bush's war against the people of
Iraq, one woman gave up her career in the U.S. diplomatic corps. Veteran
soldier and diplomat Mary Ann Wright wrote a letter to her boss, Secretary
of State Colin Powell: "This is the only time in my many years serving
America that I have felt I cannot represent the policies of an Administration
of the United States," she wrote. "I disagree with the Administration's policies on Iraq, the Israeli-Palestinian conflict, North Korea, and curtailment
of civil liberties in the U.S. itself. I believe the Administration's policies
are making the world a more dangerous, not safer, place. I feel obligated
morally and professionally to set out my very deep and firm concerns on
these policies and to resign from government service as I cannot defend or
implement them."

Ann Wright had served as Deputy Chief of Mission in U.S. embassies in Sierra Leone, Micronesia, Afghanistan, and Mongolia. She had completed assignments in Somalia, Uzbekistan, Kyrgyzstan, Grenada, and Nicaragua. She had received the State Department's Award for Heroism as charge' d'affaires during the evacuation of Sierra Leone in 1997. She had spent twenty-six years—her rank in 2003 was U.S. Army Colonel—in the U.S. Army/Army Reserves and fifteen years a diplomat. She had participated in civil reconstruction projects after military operations in Grenada, Panama and Somalia. Ann Wright resigned her State Department position in protest March 19, 2003. Two years later Ann Wright told the Pacifica news program *Democracy Now* that she had met another resister, Cindy Sheehan, at a "Veterans for Peace" conference in Dallas, Texas.

Sheehan would end up sacrificing her marriage, her health and income protesting the U.S. war in Iraq. Not far from the summer home of President Bush at Crawford, Texas, Wright and Sheehan organized Camp Casey, named in honor of Sheehan's son, Army Spc. Casey Sheehan, who had died April 4, 2004, in Baghdad, Iraq. According to the online Fallen Heroes Memorial, Casey Sheehan had been killed when his unit was fired upon by rocket-propelled grenades and small arms. The Camp Casey effort jump-started a more highly publicized U.S. anti-war movement. Wright coordinated ongoing operations at the camp. Despite verbal attacks from mostly men in mass media and other Americans on the political Left and Right, Sheehan and fellow anti-war protesters continued the Camp Casey effort through the fall and winter of 2005 and into the spring of 2007.

Cindy Sheehan had traveled, demonstrated, led discussions, given interviews. Speaking out against the U.S.-led invasion and occupation that killed her son, harmed her life and family, and the lives and families of thousands in the United States, in the Middle East, and among Coalition Forces, she had dared to question the "noble cause" for such sacrifice. But the weekend America sets aside to remember fallen soldiers, Cindy Sheehan posted a Camp Casey-farewell to America:

I have endured a lot of smear and hatred since Casey was killed and especially since I became the so-called 'Face' of the American anti-war movement …

[W]hen I started to hold the Democratic Party to the same standards that I held the Republican Party, support for my cause started to erode and the 'left' started labeling me with the same slurs that the right used. I guess no one paid attention to me when I said that the issue of peace and people dying for no reason is not a matter of 'right or left', but 'right and wrong'.

I am deemed a radical because I believe that partisan politics should be left to the wayside when hundreds of thousands of people are dying for a war based on lies that is supported by Democrats and Republicans alike.[… I have been called every despicable name that small minds can think of and have had my life threatened many times …] It amazes me that people who are sharp on the issues and can zero in like a laser beam on lies, misrepresentations, and political expediency when it comes to one party refuse to recognize it in their own party. Blind party loyalty is dangerous whatever side it occurs on …

… I have invested everything I have into trying to bring peace with justice to a country that wants neither …

The most devastating conclusion that I reached this morning … was that Casey did indeed die for nothing. His precious lifeblood drained out in a country far away from his family who loves him, killed by his own country which is beholden to and run by a war machine that even controls what we think. I have tried ever since he died to make his sacrifice meaningful. Casey died for a country which cares more about who will be the next American Idol than how many people will be killed in the next few months while Democrats and Republicans play politics with human lives …

I have also tried to work within a peace movement that often puts personal egos above peace and human life: This group won't work with that group; he won't attend an event if she is going to be there; and why does Cindy Sheehan get all the attention anyway? It is hard

> to work for peace when the very movement that is named after it has so many divisions.
>
> Our brave young men and women in Iraq have been abandoned there indefinitely by their cowardly leaders who move them around like pawns on a chessboard of destruction and the people of Iraq have been doomed to death and fates worse than death by people worried more about elections than people. However in five, ten or fifteen years our troops will come limping home in another abject defeat, and ten or twenty years from then our children's children will be seeing their loved ones die for no reason, because their grandparents also bought into this corrupt system …
>
> Camp Casey has served its purpose …

Cindy Sheehan resigned in the spring as the face-from-Camp Casey-protest but returned in the summer to out-front anti-war activism.

Continuing protests, legislation and sacrifices by Wright and Sheehan and Woolsey and Lee changed the level and content of public debate and opinion. Incremental, progressive actions have taken place within the United States. They have followed, complemented and joined worldwide protests, human rights reports, judicial and other governmental inquiries. But going against the grain is tough and few muster the courage to act counter to chauvinists in power. Standing against violence, standing for peace among warmongers and members of a Congress lacking the courage to act on their purported convictions takes character. Congresswomen Barbara Lee, Maxine Waters and Lynn Woolsey demonstrated character in standing counter to the mob and voting against continued hemorrhaging of U.S. resources to prolong an illegal, immoral, unprovoked, hostile occupation of a sovereign nation. Costs of war far outreach any conceivable gains.

The Stockholm International Peace Research Institute released a report in the middle of June 2007 showing that the U.S. Government's 2006 military spending was $528.7 billion (in 2005 U.S. dollars). Between 2001 and 2006 the U.S. Government appropriated in annual and supplemental funding $432 billion for its "global war on terrorism." The institute estimates that by the year 2016 the cost of the war on Iraq will reach $2,267 billion. The consequences of U.S. militarism in the few years 2001–2006 are staggering: burgeoning budget deficits, astronomical rises in government debt and debt servicing. Terrorism has risen dramatically in the period of excessive U.S. government military spending (2001 to 2006). Terrorism and worldwide refugees and migrations continued to rise as summer turned to fall in 2007. In SIPRI's report, lead researcher on Military Expenditure and Arms Production Elisabeth Skons said: "We know that millions of lives could be saved through basic health interventions that would cost a fraction of what the world spends on military forces every year."

Lynn Woolsey, Barbara Lee, Maxine Waters
Bring them Home

Congresswomen Waters, Woolsey, and Lee were right in their vote against more funds for war. They have earned America's respect and support for their courage as I noted in a March 25, 2007, open letter to these Members of the U.S. Congress.

The Hon. Barbara Lee, Member
The Hon. Maxine Waters, Member
The Hon. Lynn Woolsey, Member
United States House of Representatives
Rayburn House Office Building
Washington, DC 20515

I have agreed with you for the longest time—and have decried corporate media's censoring your voices—on a war with long-term consequences and immediate harm to the peoples of Iraq (in the millions of deaths and refugees), the broader Middle East, and the United States of America—indeed to the peoples of South Asia, East Africa, and even Central, Western and Eastern Europe.

The policies and actions of the United States Government in and pertaining to the Near East (invasions and occupations, arming nations and their counterparts, failing seriously to negotiate the Israeli-Palestinian conflict, irrational pro-Israel bias in the billions of dollars and lives) are reprehensible. One judge in Spain last week went so far as to call for war crimes charges to be brought against the invaders and occupiers of Iraq, which have left countless thousands dead and displaced. Not only are U.S. policies and actions causing the rise and spread of worldwide terrorism. They are simultaneously contaminating the United Nations and NATO, imperiling peaceful forces such as those through the post-Cold War European Union (now at 50), deepening dire developmental needs and crises in Africa, and forestalling any hope of progress in Africa.

In reflecting on the European Union at fifty, a British non-government official said last week on British Broadcasting that the greatest challenge facing the European Union in the next fifty years will be extending to developing countries of Africa and Asia the democracy, peace and prosperity progressively being enjoyed by countries (now twenty-seven) of the European Union.

But U. S. policies and practices that continue breaching nations' sovereignty, destabilizing geographical and political regions, trafficking in weapons, proliferating nuclear materials, fueling the arms race worldwide—all undermine justice, human freedom, and progressive efforts for generations to come. Therefore U.S. politics of the status quo, hawkishness hiding under claims of progressiveness, continued buying and selling of influence within government (earmarking, hiding payoffs in bills) and between government officials and private corporations (campaign finance versus democracy), end runs around legal and ethical processes a la Pelosi-Murtha, pliable politicians, and rabid partisanship are untenable and unacceptable in the twenty-first century.

Your stand shines the light on short-sighted, corrupt government. I applaud you. In your vote against H.R. 1591 you have demonstrated the principled power of a "majority of one," and I for one have never been prouder of Americans—American women!! Thank you for courage in the face of repressive chauvinism. You are right: You don't "win an occupation." Withholding another $100 billion and withdrawing U.S. troops are not conflicting strategies. Withdrawing U.S. troops with time lines for withdrawal and with funding already in the pipeline or designated can be achieved reasonably and safely. This *is* the right thing to do.

Yours respectfully ...

But will the history-making Speaker of the U.S. House of Representatives line up with Peace Women in Congress or will she fall in with old guard chauvinists? When California Representative Nancy Pelosi approached and ascended to the Speakership the press described her as a clothes hog known for holding grudges against congressional colleagues. But many outside federal Washington hoped she would use her new powers to sweep clean the federal legislature; at least lean in that direction. But many also worried about her apparent close association with Pennsylvania Representative John Murtha, a Member of Congress who had racked up an unclean professional record. From the 1980s' Congressional bribery scandal to his alleged continuous involvement in conflict of interest lobbying and earmarking and pay-to-play backroom Congressional maneuvers, Murtha's professional record is rife with real and perceived corruption. Contrary to popular opinion among mass media, Left and Right, Murtha was not out front in the movement against the illegal and immoral war perpetrated on the Iraqis and the Middle East. Murtha is at best a hawk interested not in bringing U.S. troops home, but in redeploying them within the Middle East. At worst he is a government insider helping to power the lucrative and insatiable machine of worldwide militarism. The hope is that the new Speaker will turn away from the Murthas whose iron fists have held to the status quo. The hope is that Speaker Pelosi will turn toward peace women and progressives in Congress. Use her power to un-censor women whom mass media have censored. Listen to their advice, take their lead, and let it enlighten the nation.

Congresswomen Barbara Lee and Lynn Woolsey have taken consistent leadership against invasion and occupation of Iraq, and for sensible withdrawal from Iraq. They have stood valiantly against a U.S. invasion of Iran. Between 2003 and 2006 Lee and Woolsey proposed several pieces of legislation aimed at disavowing the doctrine of preemptive invasion, investigating what prompted the U. S. Invasion of Iraq, repealing authorization for war, legislating against permanent Middle Eastern occupation, and developing and executing a plan for bringing U.S. troops home.

- On January 9, 2005, Rep. Barbara J. Lee introduced House Resolution 82 with fifteen cosponsors (John Murtha and Nancy Pelosi were not among them) to "disavow the doctrine of preemption."

- On January 26, 2005, Rep. Lynn C. Woolsey introduced House Congressional Resolution 35 with thirty-four cosponsors (no Murtha or Pelosi) calling on President Bush to create and carry out "a plan to begin the immediate withdrawal of United States Armed Forces from Iraq."

- On June 30, 2005, Rep. Barbara Lee introduced House Con. Res. 197 with eighty-six cosponsors (no Murtha or Pelosi) declaring U.S. policy "not to enter into any base agreement with the Government of Iraq that would lead to a permanent United States military presence in Iraq."

- On July 21, 2005, Rep. Lee introduced House Res. 375 with eighty-three cosponsors (no Murtha or Pelosi) asking President Bush and directing the Secretary of State that once the legislation had been passed they should send to the House of Representatives within fourteen days "all information in the possession of the President and the Secretary of State relating to communication with officials of the United Kingdom between January 1, 2002, and October 16, 2002, relating to the policy of the United States with respect to Iraq." [The international press had exposed the Downing Street Memo suggesting prior intent, doctoring of intelligence to justify the U.S. invasion of Iraq.]

- On July 25, 2006, Rep. Lynn Woolsey introduced H.R. 5875 with twenty-six cosponsors (no Murtha or Pelosi) "to repeal the Authorization for Use of Military Force Against Iraq Resolution of 2002 (Public Law 107–243)."

In view of Congresswomen's sensible, studied and human-centered legislative efforts—and in the face of the criminally deepening quagmire created by the Executive branch and an entrenched Congressional old guard—Speaker Pelosi would better serve her office and the country by adhering to the leadership example set by principled progressive peace women in Congress. History will tell which road was taken by the history-making Speaker of the U.S. House of Representatives.

"I always felt that my job, as designed by the founding fathers, was to listen to the people, engage their minds, stir up controversy, and steer of sanctimony ... I'm proud of the fact that I never paid for a poll ... The old-time view of politics held that the *vox populi* was important, but the person in power who has a sworn duty to lead is a little more focused than the rest of us."

Hon. Patricia Schroeder (b. 1940)
Twelve-term Member of the United States House of Representatives
(1972–1996)

From South Central LA: Waters and Millender-McDonald

Congresswoman Maxine Waters has stacked up eighteen years representing California's 35th District in the U.S. House of Representatives these years following fourteen years in the State legislature. Waters is considered one of the most powerful women bridging twentieth and twenty-first century politics in America. Her legislative efforts have had national and international import. Her activism covers a broad spectrum of issues beginning in local communities.

Congresswoman Waters' local, national, and international efforts have focused on poverty elimination, economic development, equal justice under the law and other issues concerning people of color, women, children, and poor people. She has encouraged and supported women campaigning for public office. She has crusaded for international peace, justice and human rights. While in the California legislature she worked among world leaders pushing to end South African Apartheid. In the U.S. House of Representatives in 2004 she opposed the coup d'état that overthrew Haiti's democratically-elected government of Jean-Bertrand Aristide. She has defended rights of Haitian political prisoners and led efforts in Congress to cancel debts, relieve the international debt burden, owed by poor African and Latin American countries. She is a founding member and joint leader of the 75-member "Out of Iraq Congressional Caucus" established in the summer of 2005 to heighten congressional debate on the war in Iraq and the George W. Bush administration's justifications for invading that country, and to urge the earliest possible return of U.S. service members to their families.

Waters has been Chief Deputy Whip of the Democratic Party since the 106th Congress and has co-chaired the powerful House Democratic Steering Committee. She holds membership on the Committee on the Judiciary and its subcommittees on the Courts, the Internet and Intellectual Property; on Crime, Terrorism and Homeland Security; and on Immigration, Border Security and Claims. She chaired the Democratic Caucus's Special Committee on Election Reform following the disputed 2000 presidential election. The Committee held hearings throughout the country gathering data to inform congressional deliberations on minimum federal standards in elections practices. Waters led the development of the Minority AIDS Initiative (1998) to address the alarming spread of HIV/AIDS among African Americans, Hispanics, and other minorities. Under her leadership, funding for the Minority AIDS Initiative has risen from $156 million (fiscal year 1999) to $400 million (fiscal 2006). Expanding health services for patients with diabetes, cancer and Alzheimer's are among the issues legislation authored by Congresswoman Maxine Waters.

In Memoriam: Juanita Millender-McDonald 1938–2007
Legacy in Words and Work

Twenty-four days between April and May America lost two leading American women. One was Yolanda Denise King (b. November 17, 1955, Montgomery, Alabama, d. May 15, 2007, Santa Monica, California) profiled in one of my news columns at the time. The other was Congresswoman Juanita Millender-McDonald (b. September 7, 1938, Birmingham, Alabama, d. April 21, 2007, Carson, California). Both women were Southern born, nearly a generation apart. They were progressive women who sought to educate, empower and enlighten people, including themselves, to create a better future. They left legacies in work and words worthy of remembrance and reflection.

Juanita Millender-McDonald was speaking on the Floor of the U.S. House of Representatives December 21, 2001. Her topic was Social Security and plans by the Bush administration to destroy a program that has meant the difference between poverty and survival especially for retired women, disabled people, widows and orphans.

"While all workers contribute a share of earnings in order to ensure a minimum standard of living for the elderly, disabled-workers and their families, children of deceased wage earners and surviving spouses," Millender-McDonald declared "it is women that constitute the majority of elderly Social Security beneficiaries. Approximately 60 percent of Social Security recipients are women over the age of 65 and about 72 percent of beneficiaries above the age of 85 are women."

Millender-McDonald was a smart woman who did her homework for building her case. She continued in that House speech. "Women in our nation rely heavily on Social Security as a source of income in old age: 27 percent of women over age 65 count on Social Security for 90 percent of their income. As it relates to our disabled, 37 percent of beneficiaries are disabled—they are not retired. The Social Security System was designed to provide a foundation or retirement income for disabled people and to provide protection for their families. This bill is absent on this issue."

Understanding women workers, as Justice Ginsburg had understood working women, Millender-McDonald enlightened, particularly the men, in Congress about the situation with working women. Addressing the Speaker of the House she pointed out that

> Women, on average, earn less than men, [which means] that they count on Social Security's weighted benefit structure to ensure that they have an adequate income in retirement. Women are less likely to be covered by an employer-sponsored pension plan [which] means that Social Security comprises a larger portion of their total retirement income. Women lose an average of 14 years in earnings because they take time out of the workforce to raise their children or to care for their ailing parents or spouses ... When women are in the workforce, they often work in part-time jobs; [this] means that they have less opportunity to save for retirement. Since women live six to eight years longer than men do, they must make their retirement savings stretch over longer periods of time. Consequently, women depend considerably upon Social Security's progressive, life-long, inflation-indexed benefits.

Women would be hardest hit by privatization, Millender-McDonald warned. In addition to undermining benefits to women, retired people and the disabled, privatization would disadvantage women because women generally lack knowledge or a sophisticated knowledge of the Stock Market necessary to benefit from private pension investment plans. "Many women lack the skills involved in making investment decisions, decisions that would be vital to their long-term financial security." Moreover "because women earn less, live longer and spend less time in the workforce, they will have less to invest in their private pension plan. The result would be that women would have to live on smaller benefits from smaller accounts." The core element in this warning is poverty—the continued downward spiral in feminized or institutionalized women's and children's poverty. Looking at the present and toward the future, Millender-McDonald was trying to educate and sensitize her House colleagues about the long-term consequences of taking away the livelihood of women: furthering their disempowerment.

In the spring of 2002 Juanita Millender-McDonald was speaking at a women's empowerment conference in Los Angeles. In the speech she acknowledges women's progress but spells out in great detail women's unfulfilled agenda and how to fulfill it.

While "we are grateful for the privileges and rights that we have, in comparison to our predecessors," she said, "... the struggle which our leaders started is far from over, there are still challenges that we must overcome and there are boundaries that we must cross ..."

"[Women] have greater difficulties in breaking free of poverty [Black women experience the effects of both racial and gender inequality having the least access to resources and opportunities. African-American women, in particular, constitute the majority of the poor. They are found in the lowest paid jobs and continue to bear the brunt of poverty, illiteracy and poor health, including HIV/AIDS.]." Women experience greater difficulty breaking free of poverty, she said, because of "their larger share of family and domestic responsibilities and the existing inequalities in access to education, training and opportunities in the labor markets and decision-making ... Breaking out of such a heinous cycle (lack of access, control, resources; competitive political and economic strength; influence on decision making) demands more than getting a job, acquiring training, or being approved for credit. It implies being able to carry out one's own decisions and initiatives. It implies empowerment." Political participation is essential, Millender-McDonald said.

> The empowerment of women must include their political participation, be it directly or indirectly. African American women's participation in politics is vital in order to empower, ensure the welfare, and ensure the rights of other African-American

women. In order to treat the issue of gender in the history of African American struggles for political equality one cannot just 'add women and stir.' Rather, we must incorporate women into the processes, into the political arena to support individuals and issues that address the African American community. There needs to be more policy and legislative interventions to approach the process of addressing the patent imbalances faced by women, in particular women of color ...

From where she started to where she went to what she took on as the critical issues of her time, (See also Chapter II), Congresswoman Juanita Millender-McDonald used her words and work successfully to bridge cultures, regions and nations, to deepen understanding of human issues, and to further the causes of justice, nonviolence and peaceful coexistence.

VII

World Women Policymakers, Lawmakers, Peacemakers

Five Leading Change Makers in Words and Work

Women's work and words are especially vital in an era torn by war. Wars perpetrated seemingly endlessly by profiteers, militarists, and chauvinists. Countering the tide of world militarism are some highly reputable women, moral authorities, often off center stage, heading executive and legislative offices of government, leading anti-nuclear and peace and justice efforts. These women model and inspire the kind of leadership that has potential for altering world order for the better. They are often women who themselves have been victims of militarism. Working together present to future these women will free the world from the cycle of violence, death, displacement, and despair.

Dr. Hanan Ashrawi of the Middle East

Dr. Hanan Ashrawi is a Palestinian lawmaker and peacemaker who has felt the heartaches and disappointments, the false promises and daily misery, the attempted and half-hearted peaceful resolutions to waves upon waves of crises in the Palestinian-Israeli world. She knows firsthand what it means and what it does to people to be occupied, chained in, denied work and means of supporting a family, constantly under threat and harassment. The year the planes hit the World Trade Center in New York Dr. Ashrawi spoke with David Frost on the BBC program "Breakfast with Frost." Insightfully she termed the U.S. tragedy a "moment of tremendous pain" when the world was "reconsidering where it went wrong and how we could join together in order to reaffirm our humanity."

That September 16, 2001, morning when she spoke from Ramallah this prestigious Palestinian legislator gave David Frost and viewers a firsthand account of what it means to be under siege: "To come here this morning," she said, "I had to go through shooting, my husband took his mother to chemotherapy, they had to drive through tanks and shelling, nobody slept last night, we are besieged and we are being shelled and killed and houses destroyed and by an Israeli occupation and military occupation." Later in the interview she recounted recent numbers dead and wounded: In 2000, she said. "we had over 700 Palestinians killed, civilians, and over 20,000 injured. Since the bombing, Israel has killed 24 Palestinians and wounded 200, they're all civilians. The occupation is the cause of all this and Israeli behavior has generally undermined human values, has undermined American legitimacy and credibility and has given rise to terrorism as a state terrorizing a whole population with full impunity."

Dr. Hanan Ashrawi is a leading feminist, peacemaker, thinker, and lawmaker. In addition to being a member of the Palestinian Legislative Council, she is secretary general of the Palestinian Initiative for the Promotion of Global Dialogue and Democracy. On the politics and crises in the Middle East, British Broadcasting has placed her "among the most knowledgeable, experienced and intelligent voices" in the world.

Four years after her interview with Frost—and before the 2007 massacres in Gaza—the U.S. Secretary of State had appeared on CNN praising what was hoped to be another lasting but progressive Palestinian-Israeli agreement in the Gaza. Dr. Ashrawi also appeared on that November 15, 2005, CNN segment headlined "Gaza Deal Reached."Ashrawi knew then that the agreement was half-hearted and fell short of ensuring necessary progressive measures that would enable Palestinians to live free, productive, self-governing and satisfying lives.

In the CNN-International interview Ashrawi said Palestinians had hoped for a political course that—coupled with Palestinians' promises of internal and security reforms and a quieting down period to hold elections—would include planned "negotiations to end the occupation." At the time of the interview she said Palestinians were already headed toward the exercise of their democratic rights—"if Israel would lift the siege and would allow Palestinians from Jerusalem to participate."

Instead of a full package in that 2005 "deal," Ashrawi said what the Palestinians got was "controlled access." In the U.S. Secretary of State's agreement, Ashrawi said, "Gaza and the Palestinians do not have sovereign control over the crossing points, boundaries, and so on." Israel retains total control and the consequences are "more Palestinian anger, more hostility, more victimization, more pain, and more turning to extremist elements." But if "there is some relief," she said, "if there's freedom of movement, if there is some kind of prosperity, or at least alleviation of suffering, economic and otherwise, then it means that the voices of moderation would gain more support ..." It is time "to prove that the rational, moderate political course of action will produce results."But "These results are limited."

Dr. Ashrawi concluded that "Unless the world enforces International Law and the Declaration of Human Rights there will be increasing violence and instability ... Israel has all the benefits but takes no responsibility as an occupier as stated in the Geneva Convention. Israel and the USA are perceived as the enemy and are starving the people. We are in desperate need of a viable peace process and need international intervention to control Israel ... Unless the world enforces International Law and the Declaration of Human Rights there will be increasing violence and instability." So the 2005 deal failed, as Ashrawi predicted, for being an unfair deal. In 2007 came more waves of Palestinian-Israeli-Hamas-Fatah-Gaza crises fueled, fanned and funded by U.S. and Israeli governments.

International and regional conflicts, civil, religious, racial and tribal wars, ethnic conflicts are the deepest, most piercing problems of our times. Not alone because war kills—and wounds children and women into distant generations; but because war drains. Drains people and nations of their substance: a light and liveliness, a quality of creativity in human spirit and intellect, an embracing openness, a freedom from fear that allows difference to learn from difference, to get along with diverse peoples of the world. Violence creates fear and suspicion creating more violence, more fear, and more suspicion. When the multitudes are reduced, by the few, to crumbs from the tables of the few, the multitudes rage against that oppression in whatever way they can. When the rich and powerful take disproportionately (more than their rightful share), making the many fight over scraps left by the rich, the oppressed often turn to violence—as under torture at Abu Ghraib or suicide bombing in Baghdad—furthering their own misery. Militarism (usually hand in hand with corruption) is the central, most fundamental thief of nations' treasuries.

In early July citizens of the United States learned from a June 28, 2007, nonpartisan Congressional Research Service report that the United States of America's federal government was robbing the U.S. treasury to the tune of $12 billion a month. Congress appropriated $611 billion for wars between fiscal year 2001 and May 25, 2007. At the current rate, the report said—and if Congress approves the administration's Fiscal 2008 military budget request of "$141.7 Billion for the Department of Defense's war costs, $4.6 billion for foreign and diplomatic operations, and about $800 million for VA medical costs" for continued hostilities against Iraq and a so-called Global War on Terrorism—the U.S. government will have robbed the American people of "$758 billion, including about $567 billion for Iraq, $157 billion for Afghanistan, $29 billion for enhanced security, and $5 billion unallocated."

The government is said to be allocating a third of the U.S. federal budget for war. With this flush from the treasury, government officials are not only encouraging corruption—and more wars—they are deepening suffering and deepening deficits in U.S. cities' infrastructure and democratic processes, in educational quality, access and institutions, in libraries, health care and environmental protection, wages and labor; denying the possibility of nonpartisan, non-politicized, productive ideas on critical issues such as energy and immigration and poverty elimination, ethics, human rights, and a free press in an era of irreversible globalization.

"We know that millions of lives could be saved through basic health interventions that would cost a fraction of what the world spends on military forces every year," Elisabeth Skons' words bear repeating. The Stockholm International Peace Research Institute's June 2007 report in which her warning appears breaks out the world's staggering loss to military expenditure and arms production.

- Total Nuclear Warheads held by five countries (United States of America, Russia, France, United Kingdom, China) at the start of 2007: 26,000
- Percentage of world's Military Spending vested in fifteen countries: 83 percent Military Spending 2006 in five countries (2005 dollars):
  - United States of America: $528.7 billion
  - China (biggest in Asia, fourth in the world): $49.5 billion
  - Japan: $43.7 billion
  - Russia: $34.7 billion
  - India (third highest in Asia): 23.9 billion
- United States of America & Russia: biggest arms traffickers (sellers, exporters)
- China and India: biggest arms buyers (importers, resellers)
- European Union & USA: biggest suppliers (traffickers) of arms to Middle East
- U. S. Government's annual & supplemental "Global war on terrorism" appropriations 2001–2006: $432 billion
- Cost of war on Iraq by Year 2016: $2,267 billion
- U.S. militarism 2001 forward, Consequences:
  - Deepening deficits
  - Deepening debt, rising debt servicing
  - Declining domestic infrastructure, institutions
  - Declining international diplomacy, humanitarian aid

Dr. Wangari Maathai of East Africa

The U.S. press made condescending noises when Dr. Wangari Maathai won the 2004 Nobel Peace Prize. Wangari Maathai is not only a woman but a woman who fits none of the Western male-supremacist stereotypes of woman. The press sneered because Wangari Maathai is an independent women's-rights-feminist woman. They sneered because she is a black African Ph.D.-Professor-Member of Parliament-Minister for Environment woman. The press sneered because Wangari Maathai is a scientist: environmentalist and biologist. She is a peace and justice, democracy and human rights worker who, not unlike America's own Fannie Lou Hamer, has endured great suffering in the causes of peace and justice and democracy and human rights; struggling in the great, global cause for life on Planet Earth.

Wangari Maathai's greatest contribution to the world is understanding the link between life and life: forests and humankind. She connects justice and injustice, war and peace. Maathai has devoted her life to the struggle for life. She has led a reforestation movement planting trees in the millions. If deforestation (cutting down trees, commercial logging, clear cutting, burning and damaging forests) continues at the present rate, says a NASA report, the world's rain forests will vanish within 100 years. The majority of the planet's plant and animal species will die. "When a forest is cut and burned to establish crop land and pastures," the Earth Observatory report says, "the carbon that was stored in the tree trunks ... joins with oxygen and is released into the atmosphere ... From 1850 to 1990, deforestation worldwide (including the United States) released 122 billion metric tons of carbon dioxide into the atmosphere, with the current rate being approximately 1.6 billion metric tons per year. Fossil fuel burning (coal, oil and gas) releases 6 billion metric tons of CO^2 into the atmosphere annually. Carbon dioxide in the atmosphere enhances greenhouse effect and could contribute to an increase in global temperatures." [http://earthobservatory. nasa.gov ...].

All life needs trees. "Trees protect the soil against erosion and reduce the risks of landslides and avalanches." In his 1997 article "Deforestation: Humankind and the global ecological crisis," Stephen Hui reminds that

trees help to sustain freshwater supplies and therefore are an important fac-
tor in the availability of one of life's basic needs (water). Forests affect the
climate and are an important source of oxygen. "Humankind is the cause
of deforestation." And humankind can cure it, Hui said.

Wangari Maathai won the Nobel Peace Prize because she put her back to
the wheel of reforestation by planting and leading communities in planting
millions of trees in Africa. She won it because she used her mind to make
the connection between forests and peace, justice and life; between deforestation and war, poverty and death, conditions which take particular toll on
women and children of Kenya, of Africa—of the world. "Wangari Maathai
was the first of the global leaders to say the health of our communities is
the health of the planet," commented environmental author Terry Tempest
Williams in a Pacifica interview with *Democracy Now* host Amy Goodman.
Maathai "said that environmental responsibility is social responsibility. She
was one of the first global leaders decades ago to say that there is no separa-
tion between how we treat the environment and how we treat each other,"
Williams said.

A butterfly flutters its wings on the coast of East Africa; winds, great
storms touch down in North America. Great forests fall to rubber planta-
tions, corporate cattle farms, massive Agri-businesses, and logging capital-
ists; flood waters rise, mud slides rush down slopes, waters run through
streets wiping out cities and towns, clapboard houses, trailers of poorer
people, mansions of the rich, carbon-coughing SUVs of the careless.
In richer countries taxpayers pay for cities' and states' declared states of
emergency. Taxes fund shelters for people made homeless by storms, for
merchants who lose their places of business, for businesses whose outlay
exceeds projected loss. In poorer countries (and in sectors of rich countries)
there is no such safety net. As people suffer one after another storm the
effects, worsened by deforestation, drive up their indebtedness, deepening
it—making them slaves—to developed countries such as the United States
of America. To pay down the debt they sell off their forests, compounding
the loss, condemning people to endless poverty. More hurricanes come—as
they come to Haiti with its corporate rubber (robber) barons.

Poor Haiti: the poorest nation in the Western Hemisphere. Suffering killing corporate greed, rising debt, great storms, constant meddling by foreign governments, and civil chaos (not unlike U.S.-destroyed Iraq), Haiti has, in every sense and sector, broken down. A British Broadcasting report in late September said the 2004 storm "Jeanne" caused a thousand deaths and left tens of thousands of Haitians without food and water. What's behind Haiti's stream of natural disasters? "Environmental destruction and lack of economic development," the report said. "Haiti is one of the poorest, most densely populated and most deforested countries on Earth." Lacking peaceful, unconditional human assistance Haiti is destroyed over and over again. Where is the justice in this?

Iraq and Afghanistan suffer a similar fate of plunder, devastation and debt. A 2003 article published by the Institute for War and Peace Reporting said that since the start of the war in Afghanistan, forests have been depleted by a third because people needed firewood for cooking and heating. "War, illegal hunting, deforestation and drought combined with grinding poverty," Rahimullah Samander wrote, "have had a disastrous effect on Afghanistan's wildlife, pushing some species to the verge of extinction."

In the autumn of 2004 Washington, D.C., was the site of a protest calling for the reduction or cancellation of poor countries' indebtedness to powerful countries. But there has been no serious movement in that direction. No contender in the long and monied race to hold the office of U.S. presidency has called for debt relief or reforestation of lands destroyed by corporate plunder or holdups of poor nations. The sneering press has asked no questions about environmental destruction or devastated lives. Where is the peace and justice in this? No justice, no peace. No peace. No justice. No future: only war, suffering and death for families and children.

Wangari Maathai is an environmentalist peacemaker, advocate for justice. She holds three degrees in science, including a doctorate. She was the first woman in East and Central Africa to earn a doctoral degree. She has received also several honorary doctorates, including one from Hobart & William Smith Colleges in Western New York. Wangari Maathai was born in Nyeri, Kenya. In celebration of her Nobel Peace Prize she planted a tree on nearby Mount Kenya. She leads the world in the struggle for environmental conservation, democracy and human rights. Since the 1970s Wangari Maathai has planted trees and led communities and movements in planting more than 20 million trees in Africa. The paperback edition of her book *Unbowed: A Memoir* (Knopf Publishing Group) was released in late summer 2007.

Terry Tempest Williams concluded her interview with Amy Goodman and Juan Gonzalez by saying that Wangari Maathai is a woman "who has risked everything for the environment"; that her whole life has been "a gesture of deep bows to women and children and the earth." Williams said the Nobel committee's recognition of Maathai as peacemaker gives new meaning to peace.

In announcing the committee's decision to award the 2004 Nobel Peace Prize to Wangari Maathai, some of what the head of the Norwegian Nobel committee said [reprinted at Democracy Now.org] was that

Wangari Maathai has taken a holistic approach to sustainable development that embraces democracy, human rights, and women's rights in particular. She thinks globally and acts locally ... Maathai combines science, social commitment, and active politics. More than simply protecting the existing environment, her strategy is to secure and strengthen the very basis for ecologically sustainable development.

This woman's life stands beckoning others' emulation. Wangari Muta Maathai is important among world leaders because, unlike many contemporary leaders, she looks at what is happening today and sees consequences avalanching far into the future. She sees the interlock and impact worldwide of scientific, human and natural variables on human life. She uses the entirety of her human powers to address and correct problems. She earns the Nobel Peace Prize for dedicating her life to saving ours.

Dr. Angela Merkel of Germany

In the first six months of 2007 the Federal Republic of Germany's head of state, Chancellor Angela Merkel, held two globally influential positions, in addition to head of state: president of the European Council of twenty-seven nations forming the European Union; and head of the Group of Eight (G8) industrialized (rich) nations. In a speech that year celebrating the fiftieth anniversary of the Treaties of Rome that established the European Union, Chancellor Merkel seemed to be a humanistic leader capable of seeing beyond immediate gratification; a leader capable of seeing economic, political, environmental, and societal needs as having co-equal significance. In the speech she recalled how Europe's founders thought "in terms well beyond their own generation." They thought "in terms well beyond purely economic freedoms," she said. "[They] knew that in the long run the economic and the political could not be kept separate."

To sustain the Union, she said, Europe must concentrate on its "greatest strength"—the power of freedom ... in "all its manifestations":

> Freedom to express opinions freely, even when others do not like them; freedom to believe or not to believe; freedom of enterprise; freedom of artists to create their work as they see fit; freedom of the individual in his responsibility for the whole community. [In the age of globalization] the decision in favour of Europe ... combines economic success and social responsibility ... Only together can we ensure economic and social standards also internationally. [The ingredients of progress in Union include a united foreign and security policy, cooperation in Europe and partnerships abroad; ending racism, anti-Semitism and xenophobia; then working toward] the peaceful resolution of conflicts in the world and [ensuring] that people do not become victims of war, terrorism and violence, that poverty, hunger and diseases such as AIDS are driven back ... promoting freedom and development in the world.

Chancellor Merkel grew up on the East side of the Berlin Wall. She noted this early in her EU celebratory speech and personalized the memory: "I did not believe I would ever be able to travel to the West until I was a pensioner [retired] ... But then the Wall collapsed after all ... [And] That was the defining moment for me: I realized that nothing ever has to stay the way it is." Europe's modern understanding of integration, she said, is "embedded institutional structures *instead of* [emphasis added] 'them against us' attitudes, the formation of axes and go-it-alone policies. Europe must never divide, or allow itself to be divided, over any issue."

The United States in the past several years has been painfully divided within itself and between itself and other nations of the world so that Chancellor Merkel's March 2007 speech—as Barbara Jordan's thirty years past—seemed counsel to the United States of America. America needs a spirit of unity within the Americas and an adjustment in attitude enabling it to form and retain nonviolent, respectful partnerships, particularly (though not exclusively) within the Americas and with countries of Eastern Europe, Southwest Asia, and the Horn of Africa.

Germany's first woman chancellor is also on record as the first woman and non-Catholic to lead her party, the Christian Democratic Union, and the first from the liberal wing of the Christian Democratic Union. During 2007 when Germany held the presidency of the twenty-seven nation European Union and during the Group of Eight Summit at Heiligendamm, Germany, Merkel received high marks for her leadership and negotiation skills, her constitutional focus within the EU, and pressure on other industrialized nations to confront and help curb pollution causing climate change.

Dr. Helen Caldicott of Australia and USA

The world's leading anti-nuclear figure is the physician, activist and author Helen Broinowski Caldicott. She has spent a lifetime speaking and writing on the physical effects of nuclear detonation. She opposes nuclear power for energy and for weapons purposes. Her activism against nuclear use spans decades, from her native Australia to the United States of America. It took particular hold in the late1970s in the United States when the Three Mile Island (Pennsylvania) nuclear reactor came within an hour of a possible meltdown. She led the group Physicians for Social Responsibility which had been formed in the 1960s. Dr. Caldicott has written several books, among them *Nuclear Madness: What you can do!*; *Missile Envy: the Arms Race and Nuclear War*; *If you love this planet: a plan to heal the Earth*; and *Nuclear Power is not the Answer*. She received the Australian Peace Prize in 2006 and in 1985 she was among the nominees for the Nobel Peace Prize.

Published on the website of an organization she founded, Nuclear Policy Research Institute—creating consensus for a nuclear-free future—is Helen Caldicott's "credo." In part it says she believes:

> Women have the fate of the Earth in the palm of their hands.
>
> We can save the planet.
>
> We are here to serve.
>
> We are not here to make ourselves happy, to be self-indulgent or to be hedonistic.
>
> The greatest terror in the world is not a few terrorists hitting the World Trade Center. [But] the fact that half the world's people still live in dire poverty and 30,000 to 40,000 children die every day from malnutrition and starvation, while the rich nations continue to get richer and richer.
>
> The secret to happiness is to serve our follow human beings and love and care for everyone ...; to understand our own psychology in a profound way, so we can be a more constructive human being; and to care for this incredible planet of ours.

Dr. Mary McAleese of Ireland

On April 15, 2006, the president of Ireland, Mary McAleese, was speaking to a joint meeting of Jordan's Houses of Parliament in Amman. She began in the usual way: bringing the peace, recognizing the monarchs and friendly connections between her country and Jordan. Further on President McAleese praises the neighborliness between European (European Union countries) and Mediterranean states and peoples, the latter encompassing the Middle East's Palestine, Israel, Jordan, Iraq, Iran, and others. She raises critical concerns about crises and disparities within and between states north of the Mediterranean Sea and nations south of it. In the following long excerpt from President McAleese's Amman speech, she raises critical concerns, dispels myths, corrects misstatements and errors of history, and offers humanistic solutions to crises in the Middle East:

> The widening gap between the standards of living on the northern and southern regions of the Mediterranean Sea cannot be ignored. Peace in the Middle East has not been achieved. The challenges have, if anything, become more complex and more dangerous yet all the more urgent in their need of resolution …
>
> Ignorance of one another, suspicion of one another, fear, misconceptions, mutual incomprehension these are now the highly combustible fuel that ignites conflict and energises the pernicious myth that our cultures, our faiths and civilisations are inherently incompatible … [This] myth is susceptible to exploitation, with horribly tragic consequences. At every level it is clear that we have to invest in developing and enriching our peoples' understanding of each other. We have to reveal through our efforts the joy, wonder, progress, prosperity and peace that flow from respectful acceptance of our diversity and from partnership with one another."

Acknowledging the Islamic World's anger and hurt resulting from mass media's publication of images purporting to characterize or mischaracterize the Prophet Mohammed, she urged conciliation. "I believe," she said, "we all now have an obligation to re-examine our relationships and to ensure that they are based on, and at all times reflect, a real sense of respect for each other's deeply-held values, beliefs, cultures and traditions." She continued with a historical Middle East/Northeast Africa reference that is rarely spoken in the West:

> The story of European civilisation cannot be told without considerable mention of this region as the cradle of culture and philosophy which moulded so much that we take for granted in our daily life. Every true European knows that our heritage is incomprehensible without reference to towns and cities such as Baghdad, Jerusalem, Nazareth, Bethlehem, Cairo, Alexandria

and historic Petra. To attempt to un-bundle, to separate our cultures as if they were no more than parallel but separate universes, would be to rewrite history. We are wound together like strands of a rope—pull us apart and we still bear each others imprint for we have shaped one another indelibly. Whatever the vanities of history we know they cannot be undone but we can prevent the future from becoming another wasted opportunity, a landscape of wasted lives. We have a clear and pressing obligation to build new bridges between our peoples and to invigorate the links between Europe and the Middle East …

President McAleese pledged that Ireland with the EU would work with Middle Eastern leaders and "with the Iraqi people in fulfillment of our collective responsibility under the Charter of the United Nations to build a prosperous future for Iraq based on inclusiveness, democracy and respect for human rights." Pointing to the Arab-Israeli conflict, she said it "has for too long blighted too many lives in this region." And though "international experts and commentators" have characterized the conflict "as the ultimate insoluble problem, such a counsel of despair simply cannot be allowed to prevail."

We must assert with conviction that it is possible, indeed it is essential, to effect a settlement which will bring peace to Israel, Palestine, Syria and Lebanon.

What links these leading change makers—Hanan Ashrawi, Wangari Maathai, Angela Merkel, Helen Caldicott, Mary McAleese—is their unambiguous support for nonviolence, justice, respect for and understanding of and among nations and peoples, international humanitarian uplift and cooperation, peaceful coexistence among peoples—and with Planet Earth.

VIII

Women Political Decision Makers Worldwide

Women are slightly more than half the world's population, Farzana Bari wrote in a November 3, 2005, paper for the United Nations Division for the Advancement of Women. By virtue of their dual roles in productive and reproductive spheres, "[Women's] contribution to the social and economic development of societies is also more than half [the contribution] of men. Yet their participation in formal political structures and processes where decisions are made regarding the use of societal resources generated by both men and women remains *insignificant* [emphasis added]. [Women's] representation in legislatures around the world is 15 percent …"Only in twelve countries are women holding "33 percent or more seats in the parliaments [legislatures]." The 2006 United Nations Commission Report on the Status of Women recalled General Assembly resolution 58/142 of 2003 urging all countries "to develop a comprehensive set of programs and policies to increase women's participation, especially in political decision making." The report also reaffirmed earlier Commission recommendations to implement strategies promoting "gender balance in political decision-making."

Sweden in 1999 was the first country to seat more female than male ministers: eleven women, nine men. Nineteen of the one hundred and ninety-two United Nations member countries (including Denmark, The Netherlands and United Kingdom monarchs) and two independent states outside the UN in 2007 had women government and state leaders. Women presidents presided in eight countries: Chile, Finland, Ireland, Israel (Acting), Latvia, Liberia, The Philippines and Switzerland. Women prime ministers led five countries: Germany (Chancellor), Jamaica, New Zealand, Mozambique and The Netherlands Antilles. France, according to the May 18, 2007, edition of the International Herald *Tribune*, had "one of the highest levels of women ministers of any country in Europe." While the people of the United States of America have elected some female governors, state and federal legislators, they have never elected a woman to the head the top federal executive office: the office of President of the United States.

World Women Heads of State (non-monarchs) 2007

Hon. Mary McAleese (1997–), President of Ireland: Former law professor, university administrator, journalist; "concerned with justice, equality, social inclusion, anti-sectarianism, reconciliation." B. 1951.

Hon. Dr. Dame C. Pearlette Louisy (1997–), Governor-General of St. Lucia: Former civil servant. B. 1946.

Hon. Vaira Vike-Freiberga (1999–), President of Latvia: Former university professor in Canada, leadership in Science Council of Canada, later Latvian Institute in Riga; Grew up in refugee camps in Germany, schooled in French Morocco, university in Canada. B. Latvia, 1937.

Hon. Helen Clark (1999–), Prime Minister of New Zealand: Former Member of Parliament, minister of housing and conservation, deputy premier and health and labor minister. B. 1950.

Hon. Tarja Halonen (2000–), President of Finland (Finland's Prime Minister: also a woman, Anneli Jäätteenmäki, 2003–): Former Member of Parliament, several former positions at minister level: health and social affairs, Nordic co-operation, justice, foreign affairs. B. 1943.

Hon. Gloria Macapagal-Arroyo (2001–), Executive President of the Philippines: Former positions include trade and industry, social development and welfare secretary, foreign affairs, senator, vice president. B. 1947.

Hon. Anne Green (2003–), Chief Islander of Tristan da Cunha (St. Helena, British territory in the South Atlantic, Southwest of Africa): Former Chief Islander Administrator, representative of the British Governor of St. Helena. B. unknown.

Hon. Luísa Días Diogo (2004–) Prime Minister of Mozambique: Formerly in ministry of finance, ministry of planning and finance, vice minister, World Bank. B. 1958.

Hon. Nassimah Magnolia Dindar (2004–), President of the governing General Council of Réunion (French territory in Indian Ocean, East of Madagascar): Former vice president of the Regional Council. B. 1960.

Hon. Marie-Noëlle Thémereau (2004–), President of the Government of Nouvelle Caledonie (Territoire de la Nouvelle-Calédonie et Dépendances, French Territory in the southwestern Pacific east of Australia): Former vice president, Leader of l'Avenir ensemble. B. 1950.

Hon. Deborah Barnes Jones (2004–), Governor of Montserrat (Emerald Isle, British territory in the east Caribbean Sea off the north coast of Venezuela): Former positions as ambassador to Georgia also Ecuador, foreign and commonwealth office staff. B. 1956.

Hon. Michaëlle Jean (2005–), Governor-General of Canada: Former university professor, social activist, journalist. B. 1957.

Hon. Angela Merkel (2005–), Chancellor of Germany: Former minister level positions for women and youth, environment, protection of nature and reactor safety; secretary general and parliamentary leader. B. 1954.

Hon. Aili Keskitalo (2005–), President of the Sami Parliament of Norway: (Head of the Parliament and the Executive of the Sami Entity in Norway), chairperson of Norske Samers Riksforbund (National Union of Norwegian Sami). B. 1968.

Hon. Ellen Johnson-Sirleaf, (2006–), Executive President of Liberia: Former Secretary of State, of Finance, Minister of Finance, President of the National Bank, staff of the World Bank, African Director of the UNDP (United Nations Development Program). B. 1938.

Hon. Michelle Bachelet Jeria (2006–), Executive President of Chile: Former minister of health and defense; Daughter of a General killed by Pinochet (Augusto Pinochet Ugarte); Suffered (she and her mother) detention and torture under the Pinochet regime; Exiled in East Germany and Australia. B. 1952.

Hon. Portia Simpson-Miller (2006–), Prime Minister of Jamaica, Member of Parliament: Former deputy president of People's National Party, at minister level of labor, social welfare and sports, local government, community development, defense; acting prime minister. B. 1946.

Hon. Emily de Jongh-Elhage (2006–), Minister-President of Nederlandse Antillen (Dutch Nederlandse Antillen, five islands in the Caribbean Sea, an autonomous part of the Kingdom of The Netherlands): Former at commissioner level of public works and public housing, education, sport and cultural affairs, public enterprises and public housing, at minister level of education and culture, of general affairs, and external relations. B. 1946.

Hon. Micheline Calmy-Rey (2007–), President of the Confederation of Switzerland: Former president of the Grand Council (legislature) of Geneva and vice and president of the Cantonal (executive) Government of Geneva, and federal foreign minister. B. 1945.

Hon. Dalia Itzik (2007–), Acting President of Israel: Former deputy mayor of Jerusalem, at minister level of environment, trade and industry, communication. B. 1952.

Hon. Borjana Kristo (2007–), President of the Federation of Bosnia (Bosnia-Herzegovina): Former minister of justice of the Bosniak-Croat Federation, vice president of the Parliament, a vice president of the Federation. B. 1949.

Hon. Pratibha Patil (2007–), President of India: Former lawmaker, 45-year member of India's Congress Party, early party of former Prime Minister (1966–1977) Indira Gandhi, lawyer, former deputy speaker of India's upper house of Parliament, former state (Rajasthan) governor. As president she forms state and federal governments, acts as supreme commander of armed forces (army, navy, air force), grants pardons and reduces, especially death penalty, sentences [July 21, 2007, http://news.bbc.co.uk]. B. 1934.

World Women's Percentages: High Legislative, Executive Government 2007

Writing in 2006 from the Rwandan capital, Kigali, Laurie Goering reported that women in Rwanda headed the Supreme Court, held half the judgeships, and constituted half the college graduates. "A new constitution for the first time set aside 30 percent of the country's legislative seats for [women]" and "the country now has a high enough percentage of women in office … to push through controversial reforms." Rwanda has achieved the record previously held by Sweden and Norway; it now leads the world in the highest percentage of women lawmakers. A decade after the100-day

Rwandan massacre that left more than 800,000 people dead, including women who had been killed, humiliated, persecuted and sexually abused, Gumisai Mutume writes, women in Rwanda lead "the world rankings of women in national parliaments": 49 percent compared to a world average of 15.1 percent.

"Liberia now has Africa's first elected woman president, Mozambique and SaoTome and Principe have female prime ministers, and South Africa and Zimbabwe have female vice presidents," Laurie Goering reported in 2006. "Zambia has a woman running for president, Tanzania has a female foreign minister, and women hold at least 30 percent of the legislative seats in Burundi, South Africa and Mozambique."

But women still fall short of holding high government offices proportionate to their numbers and needs. In March of 2006, a United Nations report noted that "Millions of women around the world, including those in the UK and other Western countries, are being denied effective representation because of the low numbers of female politicians, judges and employers." Then-UN Secretary General Kofi Annan said, "Women are every bit as affected as any man by the challenges facing humanity in the 21st Century—in economic and social development, as well as in peace and security—often they are more affected."

Higher Executive Percentages

French Community Government (Belgium): Government members/cabinet: 4 women, 2 men (60 percent).

Chile: Ministers: 10 women, 10 men (+ the president) (50/52 percent). Subsecretaries: 15 women, 16 men (48 percent).

Spain: Government members/cabinet: 8 women, 9 men (47 percent).

South Africa: Government members/cabinet: 13 women, 15 men (46 percent). Deputy Ministers: 10 women, 11 men (47 percent).

Wales (United Kingdom): Government members/cabinet: 4 women, 5 men (45 percent).

Norway: Government members/cabinet: 9 women, 11 men (45 percent). State Secretaries: 19 women, 23 men (44 percent).

Nicaragua: Ministers/Cabinet: 45 percent women. Total government positions: 36 percent women.

Netherlands Antilles: Government members/cabinet: 4 women, 5 men (44.4 percent).

Finland: Government members/cabinet: 8 women, 11 men (42 percent).

Ecuador: Ministers: 7 women, 10 men (41.1 percent).

Sweden: Ministers: 9 women, 13 men (40.9 percent).

Austria: Government members/cabinet including State Secretaries: 40 percent women.

Montserrat (United Kingdom): Government members/cabinet: 2 women, 3 men (40 percent).

United Kingdom: Government members/cabinet: 8 women, 15 men (34.7 percent). Junior ministers: 22 women of 90 (24.4 percent).

Iceland: Government members/cabinet: 4 women, 8 men (33.3 percent).

Denmark: Government members/cabinet: 6 women, 13 men (31 percent).

Netherlands: Ministers: 5 women, 11 men (31 percent). Total women including the State Secretaries: 34 percent.

Bolivia: Ministers: 5 women, 12 men (29 percent). Vice Ministers: 1 woman, 39 men (2.5 percent).

Germany: Government members/cabinet: 6 women, 10 men (26 percent). State Ministers and Parliamentary State Secretaries: 6 women, 20 men (23 percent).

Rwanda: Government members/cabinet: 9 women, 22 men (25 percent).

Italy: Ministers: 6 women, 20 men (23 percent).

Canada: Government members/cabinet: 7 women, 25 men (21 percent).

Luxembourg: Government members/cabinet: 3 women, 12 men (20 percent).

France: Government members/cabinet: 9 women, 34 men (20 percent).

Ireland: Government members/cabinet: 3 women, 12 men (20 percent). Ministers of State: 1 woman, 14 men (7 percent).

Belgium: Government members/cabinet: 4 women, 17 men (19 percent).

Liechtenstein: Government members/cabinet year 2000 data: women 20 percent.

Source: 2007 Data Source: Worldwide Guide to Women in Leadership

Lower Executive Percentages

Afghanistan: Government members/cabinet: 1 woman.

Pakistan: Government members/cabinet: 1 woman, 32 men (3 percent). State Ministers: 5 women, 26 men. Parliamentary Secretaries: 10 women, 39 men. Advisors: 1 woman, 3 men.

Kuwait: Ministers: 1 woman, 23 men (4.1 percent).

United Arab Emirates: Government members/cabinet: 2 women, 21 men (8.6 percent).

Saint Lucia: Cabinet Ministers: 0 women, 12 men. Junior Ministers: 1 woman, 4 men.

Qatar: Ministers: 1 woman, 20 men (4.7 percent).

Oman: Ministers: 2 women, 36 men (5.2 percent).

Yemen: Ministers: 2 women, 33 men (5.7 percent).

Cambodia; Government members/cabinet: 10 women, 170 men (5.8 percent).

Angola: Ministers: 7 percent women. Vice ministers: 22 percent.

Laos: Ministers: 2 women, 26 men (7.1 percent).

Bahrain: Government members/cabinet: 2 women, 24 men (7.6 percent).

India: Government members: 8 women or 9.6 percent of 83 members. National parliament: 17 percent, federal cabinet 10 percent, average number of candidates under 10 percent. First president: July 2007.

Iraq: Ministers: 3 women, 34 men (8.8 percent).

Israel: Ministers: 2 women, 23 men (8 percent).

Vietnam: Ministers: 3 women, 27 men (10 percent).
Haiti: Government members: 2 women, 17 men (10.5 percent).

Australia: Ministers: 4 women, 25 men (13 percent).

Democratic Republic of Congo (Kinshasa): Ministers and Vice-Ministers: 9 women, 52 men (14 percent).

United States of America: Government members/cabinet: 3 women, 17 men (15 percent).

Source: 2007 Data Worldwide Guide to Women in Leadership

IX

Briefly Noted Words

Liberian President Ellen Johnson-Sirleaf

"THE GROWING NUMBER OF WOMEN IN POWER IN AFRICA
WILL IN TIME BRING PROGRESS."

In 2005 Ellen Johnson-Sirleaf was elected Liberia's first woman head of state and Africa's first elected woman president. She had been a World Bank economist. Commenting on her election results President Johnson-Sirleaf told the press, "Everyone concluded that men had ruled the country for over 100 years and had failed." January 16, 2007, at the end of Johnson-Sirleaf's first year in office, *Deutsche Welle* reported that her administration had produced free education in government-run elementary schools, which had caused a dramatic rise in school attendance; supplied electricity and water to a large part of the capital city, Monrovia; built and reconditioned roads; and increased investor confidence.

German Chancellor Angela Merkel

"WHEN WE IN EUROPE CAN SHOW THAT ECONOMICS AND ECOLOGY ARE
COMPATIBLE, THEN WE WILL HAVE DEMONSTRATED THAT WE CAN COMBINE
TECHNOLOGICAL LEADERSHIP AND INNOVATION WITH OUR RESPONSIBIL-
ITY TOWARD THE REST OF THE WORLD ... WE HAVE TO DO EVERYTHING
IN ORDER TO ISSUE A WAKE-UP CALL TO ALL NATIONS. CLIMATE CHANGE IS
ONE OF THE GREAT CHALLENGES OF THE 21ST CENTURY."

Credentialed in science, university teaching and politics, Dr. Merkel in 2005 became Germany's first woman chancellor. The *Economist* news magazine wrote in its January 13, 2007, issue that Chancellor Merkel is "one of the few EU leaders able to translate national power into international influence. She has built a reputation for herself among European peers as a straight-shooter who is consistent in her views ..." As Germany ended its six-month EU presidency in June 2007 *Deutsche Welle* again praised Merkel's negotiation skills noting that, at home and abroad, she has been "celebrated politically" as "Miss World."

Chilean President Michelle Bachelet

> "THE MOST IMPORTANT THING ... IS TO FOCUS ON LIFE,
> FREEDOM, DIGNITY AND PEACE."

Michelle Bachelet was elected President of Chile in 2006. She won the election with 53 percent of the vote. She is Chile's first woman president, the first popularly elected South American woman president who established her political career independent of her husband. She is socialist and agnostic. Exiled from her country in the 1970s, she lived and studied medicine in Australia and East Germany. Before becoming president Bachelet had risen through the ranks of party and executive governmental leadership.

During the rule of General Augusto Pinochet thousands of Chileans were detained and tortured by secret police. Bachelet was among them. In 1975 she and her mother were detained at Villa Grimaldi detention center outside Santiago, Chile. In later years the Villa Grimaldi center became a peace park to memorialize thousands of prisoners who had been tortured. Bachelet visited the park in October of 2006. During that visit she responded philosophically to a BBC interviewer: "We were the privileged ones," she said, "because we were lucky enough to survive [when thousands] of Chileans, among them my father and so many other loved ones, did not survive prison or torture." Reflecting on the past and looking forward, she acknowledged moments of sadness but added: "the most important thing about this visit is to focus on life, freedom, dignity and peace."

Finland President Tarja Halonen

> "I WANT TO BE EVERYBODY'S PRESIDENT AND I AM GOING
> TO DO MY BEST TO BECOME THAT."

Finland President Tarja Halonen seems to have been echoing, in a comment to the press, 1972 U. S. presidential candidate Shirley Chisholm. Reflecting on her presidential win Halonen said the election results show "that women as well as men can achieve any political position in our country, but there is still a lot to do before the same equality is achieved within all other areas."

In 2000 Finland elected—and in 2006 reelected—its first female president, Tarja Halonen, of the Social Democratic Party. In 2003 Finland Anneli Jäätteenmäki of the Center Party was appointed prime minister. These election results made Finland the first European nation to seat women as president *and* prime minister.

Kenyan Member of Parliament, Nobel Peace Laureate Wangari Maathai

> "PEACE ON EARTH DEPENDS ON OUR ABILITY TO SECURE
> OUR LIVING ENVIRONMENT."

In a *Democracy Now* interview Dr. Maathai recalled her advice to Kenyan women at the start of the environmental movement she led and which has seen more than 30 million seedlings planted in Kenya and a spinoff-movement spawn throughout Africa: "Use your woman sense. These tree seedlings are very much like the seeds you deal with—beans and maize and millet—every day."

U.S. Governor Christine Gregoire

> "I'M GOING TO DO MY JOB."

The election was a photo-finish, a tough call, a results-challenged Washington State race. Governor Gregoire stood her ground and won. "It was a bit of a challenge giving an inaugural address when you're looking at some members of the legislature who as of that day refused to recognize me as governor," she said in an interview with the *Economist*. "But I decided that if I'm here for six months or four years, I'm going to do my job."

French Presidential Contender Segolene Royal

"In any democracy, the people who vote are sovereign and free"

By early 2007 Segolene Royal was an established politician. In the spring she was leading the race to succeed then-President of France, Jacques Chirac. She had won the primary election with more than 60 percent of the vote. As the general election (the final round) approached she distinguished herself in candidate debates. Election results showed that Royal had beaten poll estimates by 15 percent and had come within six percentage points of becoming the first woman president of France.

Reporting for *Reuters*, Kerstin Gehmlich said Royal was a veteran in politics who had run as a fresh face out to rebuild politics of the Left, using "straight-forward language and old-fashioned glamour." The approach had impressed "many voters who [had] grown tired of a generation of male leaders cast from the same elitist mold." Though Royal observed during the course of the campaign that "No man with my professional background would have had his competence and legitimacy permanently called into question," the seating of the new government showed she had helped boost the influence of her party.

Navajo Presidential Contender Lynda Lovejoy

"People want a change in the way our government is functioning ..."

Government Commissioner Lynda Lovejoy August 2006 was running for the presidency of the Navajo Nation. Lovejoy's candidacy made history as the first time a woman had been a candidate for the presidency of the largest Native American Nation. She continues in her position as head of New Mexico's Public Regulation Commission. During her race for the top executive office she observed that her nomination suggested that "people want a change in the way our government is functioning …

"We have regressed over the last several years because we've been caught up in the appearance of progress … We are growing in population, yet our communities are stagnant, our industries have not kept up with new and advanced technology, and our workforce has declined."

Guatemalan Presidential Candidate Rigoberta Menchu

IF SHE WINS THE ELECTION THIS NOBEL PEACE LAUREATE (1992) WILL BECOME HER COUNTRY'S FIRST WOMAN PRESIDENT.

In early 2007 Rigoberta Menchu announced her candidacy for the office of President of Guatemala. Elections were scheduled for September. If she wins the election she will become the country's first woman president and its first president from Guatemala's indigenous Mayan community.

Rigoberta Menchu survives parents who were among 200,000 Maya (Mesoamerican Indians) slaughtered or caused to disappear during Guatemala's civil war. Half the country's population are said to be descendants of the Maya. Rigoberta Menchu is a long-time activist for indigenous rights and women's rights.

Rwandan Senator Odette Nyiramilimo

Her provocative words though briefer than brief and muted with "kind of" are nevertheless empowering in their brevity.

"WE ARE HAVING A KIND OF REVOLUTION"

"Peace we want because there is another war to fight against poverty, disease and ignorance. We have promises to keep to our people of work, food, clothing, and shelter, health and education."

Four-term (1966–77; 1980–1984) Prime Minister of India, Indira Priyad Arshini Gandhi (b. 1917, d. 1984)

X

World Peace Women Altering World Order

Nobel Women

W omen have been makers of peace for as long as they have lived on the planet. Yet on the one hundredth anniversary of the Nobel Peace Prize in 2001, women had received but a tenth of Nobel's awards for Peace. Four women had received individual prizes: Baroness Bertha Sophie Felicita Von Suttner of Prague (1905), Mother Teresa of India (1979), Aung San Suu Kyi of Burma (1991), and Rigoberta Menchu of Guatemala (1992). Six more prizes had been awarded to women as part of a group or joint prize. Many peace women were ignored. Among them were Hanan Ashrawi who directed the Palestinian Initiative for the Promotion of Global Dialogue and Democracy; Mary Robinson who was United Nations High Commissioner for Human Rights and the seventh president of Ireland; Mary Brownell, president of the Liberian Women's Initiative, who helped secure Liberia's disarmament and a lasting cease fire; former U.S. Congresswoman Elizabeth Furse who founded the Black Sash, a women's anti-apartheid group, and the Oregon Peace Institute and worked for human rights, peace, justice, environmental responsibility and treaty rights for Native Americans; Maya Angelou for celebrating women in all of their diversity and strength; Lani Guinier and Angela Davis for deep thinking, rights advocacy, distinguished teaching, tireless truth-speaking to power. If not these, others.

By 2003 the number of women recipients of the Nobel Peace Prize was growing. Shirin Ebadi received the prize that year. She was the eleventh woman recipient. In presenting the prize, the Norwegian Nobel Committee said Shirin Ebadi's "principal arena is the struggle for basic human rights ... In an era of violence, she has consistently supported non-violence," the

131

committee said. "It is fundamental to her view that the supreme political power in a community must be built on democratic elections. She favours enlightenment and dialogue as the best path to changing attitudes and resolving conflicts."

This lawyer, lecturer, writer, activist Nobel Peace Laureate was Iran's first woman judge; the first Iranian and third Muslim recipient of the prize. And these were just two of her firsts: She is a seriously thoughtful social activist who knows the meaning of liberty, democracy, civil rights (and what it means to be denied liberty, democracy, civil rights)—concepts often mouthed and thrown about but misunderstood, misconstrued, or taken for granted by Americans. In an interview reported in *Time* Magazine in the fall of 2003 Ebadi suggested that the U.S. government "is so busy demanding that Iran embrace democracy that it shouts over the heads of millions of Iranians who demand democracy and freedom—often at great peril. Every nation needs to select what's best for itself on its own," she told *Time*—"whether that's Iran or Iraq or in Europe."

Echoed in the life of Shirin Ebadi is a woman who received the prize before her, Aung San Suu Kyi (1991). In the struggle for freedom, justice and democracy in Myanmar, Aung San Suu Kyi said: "You should not let your fears prevent you from doing what you know is right. Not that you shouldn't be afraid. Fear is normal. But to be inhibited from doing what you know is right, that is what is dangerous. You should be able to lead your life in the right way—despite your fears."

Noting in 2006 that a hundred years of Nobel Peace Prize awards had gone to only twelve women, Laureates Jody Williams, Shirin Ebadi, Wangari Maathai, Rigoberta Menchú Tum, Betty Williams and Mairead Corrigan Maguire, women representing four continents and the Middle East, formed the Nobel Women's Initiative. Its aim was "to address and work to prevent the root causes of violence by spotlighting and promoting the efforts of women's rights activists, researchers and organizations working to advance peace, justice and equality."

The Initiative's distinguishing methods of operation are rooted in cooperation that supplements and enhances other women's efforts instead of competing with or racing against other women's efforts. Their activist mission is to bring women together. The organization's website says the Nobel Women's Initiative is concerned with "building a culture of peace:" a culture committed "to equality and justice—a democratic world free of physical, economic, cultural, political, religious, sexual and environmental violence and the constant threat of these forms of violence [particularly] against women, [generally] against all of humanity." The group held its first conference in the spring of 2007. Seventy five women researchers and activists were invited to the Galway, Ireland, meeting. Its main focus: the Middle East.

Global Women

"Women have always understood that peace requires building a broad consensus that is rooted in respect for diversity," the Global Fund for Women affirms on its Internet site. As the crisis worsened the summer of 2006 in the Middle East, the Global Fund for Women called on the United Nations and on all nations of the international community including liberation groups to change their actions, attitudes and approaches. The Global Fund for Women called for:

- Affirming the commitment to peace by abiding by the core agreements of international civil society.

- Recognizing and using regional and local women's peace groups' skills and expertise as valuable resources in mediating and resolving conflicts.

- Standing firmly against violence and unilateralism in order to promote all people's long-term human security.

- Directing resources away from military spending towards efforts that strengthen human rights with investments in the education, health and well-being of ... people.

- Rethinking the endless 'war on terror' around the world.

- Reclaiming the United Nation's position as an independent, international institution representing the whole world—not merely the leading industrial or economic powers.

- Working with Israel's and the Palestinian people's legally elected governments to end violence on all sides and peacefully to resolve conflict within the framework of international law.
- Listening to voices opposing abuse of force.

Women from the Wilderness

We were still mourning seven lives lost in space. As we mourned those dead, Washington was pushing stealthily for what had become by 2006 a sweeping massacre of hundreds of thousands of people. Few voices of peace were aired (print or broadcast) by corporate media that winter of 2003. Directly and indirectly the few voices of peace that could be heard from the wilderness formed a special bond, anchoring sanity.

Radio for Peace International crackled through shortwave. It was a global messenger carrying peace and hope to the farthest reaches of the earth. Its broadcast aimed at "creating peace in hearts, homes, communities, and all nations of the world." *Voices in the Wilderness* was working to end economic sanctions and military warfare against "ordinary Iraqis." *Vote No War* posted an open referendum calling people to sign on. The referendum text minced no words: "Thousands will die needlessly unless the people stop this war drive ... [Join] with millions of people who believe that the [now far exceeded] $200 billion planned for war against Iraq should be spent instead to fund jobs, education, housing, health care, child care, assistance to the elderly and to meet people's needs."

Also among the peace advocates, protesters and war resisters that winter 2003 were early calls on the U.S. House of Representatives to *vote a bill of impeachment* for high crimes and misdemeanors committed by the president and vice president of the United States and then-serving Defense Secretary Donald H. Rumsfeld and U.S. Attorney General John D. Ashcroft. Some of the proposed charges included:

Authorizing, ordering and condoning assassinations, summary executions, kidnapping, secret and other illegal detentions of individuals, torture and physical and psychological coercion of prisoners to obtain false statements … Violations and subversions of the Constitution of the United States of America in an attempt to commit with impunity crimes against peace and humanity and war crimes in 'pre-emptive' wars, … and threats of aggression against Afghanistan, Iraq and other nations by assuming powers of an imperial executive who is not accountable to law and usurping powers of the Congress, the Judiciary and the people of the United States …; [and] Violations and subversions of the Charter of the United Nations and international law in an attempt to commit with impunity crimes against peace and humanity and war crimes in wars and threats of aggression against Afghanistan, Iraq and others and usurping powers of the United Nations …

International Women's Day 2003 approached. The Bush government's plans to invade Iraq seemed unstoppable. And the *Women's International League for Peace and Freedom* made a promise to the women of Iraq. Their pledge mailed to Iraqi women said in part: "We pledge to do everything within our power to prevent further suffering for you, your children, and all of the Iraqi people. We call on women everywhere to join in nonviolent action to end current military operations and prevent future attacks. We are committed to doing the same. We offer whatever support we can provide, directly to you, in these very dark and dangerous days."

In the years between 2003 and 2007 scores of American women from the wilderness made deep sacrifices. Among them were Cindy Sheehan, Mary Ann Wright, Rachel Corrie, and Alice Walker.

Retired Colonel Mary A. Wright was the most senior among three U.S. diplomats who in 2003 resigned their positions over concerns about the content and direction of U.S. foreign policy (See also Wright and Sheehan, Camp Casey, Antiwar in Chapter VI). She had been deputy chief of mission at the U.S. Embassy in Mongolia. As a soldier and diplomat her resignation letter was remarkable in its overt opposition to U.S. policies on the Israeli-

Palestinian conflict, on North Korea, on U.S. civil liberties, and on Iraq. In the letter reproduced on the Internet by *Independent* Media, Wright wrote to her boss, Secretary of State Colin Powell. "All my life," she wrote, "I have been in service to the United States. I have been a diplomat for fifteen years and the Deputy Chief of Mission in our Embassies in Sierra Leone, Micronesia, Afghanistan (briefly) and Mongolia. I have also had assignments in Somalia, Uzbekistan, Kyrgyzstan, Grenada and Nicaragua. I received the State Department's Award for Heroism as charge´ d'affaires during the evacuation of Sierra Leone in 1997. I was 26 years in the U.S. Army/Army Reserves and participated in civil reconstruction projects after military operations in Grenada, Panama and Somalia. I attained the rank of Colonel during my military service. This is the only time in my many years serving America that I have felt I cannot represent the policies of an Administration of the United States."

Wright anchored her opposition to the war policy in her considerable Foreign Service credentials:

> In our press for military action now, we have created deep chasms in the international community and in important international organizations. Our policies have alienated many of our allies and created ill will in much of the world ... [The] policy and implementation of 'preemptive attack' against Iraq ... will be used against us and provide justification for individuals and groups to 'preemptively attack' America and American citizens.

She concluded her letter by saying that she had served her country "for almost thirty years in some of the most isolated and dangerous parts of the world." That she wanted "to continue to serve America." But that she did not believe "in the policies of this Administration and [could] not defend or implement them." It was, she said, "with heavy heart that I must end my service to America and therefore resign ..."

But that was not quite the end of diplomat Mary Wright's service to the United States of America. Two years after her resignation, in August 2005, she was running Camp Casey near the summer home of President George W. Bush. Camp Casey had been established at Crawford, Texas, with anti-war activist Cindy Sheehan, the mother of a U.S. soldier who had died in Washington's war on Iraq. Mothers and others at the camp were memorializing their war dead (sons and daughters) and calling on the U.S. president to meet with them and give a just cause for their sons' and daughters' deaths.

Interviewing on the morning of August 19, 2005, as she was running "Field Operations for Peace" at Crawford, Texas, Ann Wright was ecstatic. She told *Democracy Now's* Amy Goodman that they were "setting up field operations, for peace, not war." Starting "with one car staying overnight, one tent, two tents, three tents," she said. "Now we have got … 80 cars and about 40 tents that stayed the night here. And during the course of the day, we'll be having probably 300 to 400 people that will be coming through from all over the country to spend a couple of hours, maybe a day or two. It's a remarkable outpouring from America."

A year later as the country became more and more paranoid, Ann Wright came up against the hard-edged U.S. military in a leafleting incident. This retired Colonel and diplomat was at Fort McNair handing out material on a documentary, "Sir, No Sir: The Suppressed Story of a GI Movement to End the War in Vietnam." For this act, military workers detained this distinguished officer, handcuffing her to a chair for the better part of a day. Neither she nor Cindy Sheehan has finished protesting the government's unprovoked attacks on foreign nations and peoples and the use of Americans as fodder in those hostilities.

Rachel Corrie stood in front of a Caterpillar bulldozer in the Gaza Strip trying to protect the homes and lifeline of Palestinians being destroyed by Israelis. News reports said the driver of that army vehicle saw her clearly as she was dressed in bright-colored clothing, the kind of clothing worn by crossing guards and road workers. But the bulldozer driver ran her down. Rolled over her and killed her—dead. Rachel Corrie was an American whose government sponsors war and injustice against the Palestinians (and against Rachel) through propaganda, political bias, arms and financial support of the Israeli government. Rachel Corrie was twenty-three years old when they killed her.

Her mother told British Broadcasting reporters that Rachel Corrie had spent nights sleeping at wells to protect Palestinians from bulldozers. But her daughter had been "a committed peace activist even before her arrival in the Gaza Strip" a few months before they murdered her that late winter Sunday (March 16, 2003). She had seen Palestinians bearing up under unbearable conditions and genocide. She had been heartened by their struggle; shaken by the world's indifference. Writing to her parents she said:

> [A] lot of the time the sheer kindness of the people here, coupled with the overwhelming evidence of the wilful destruction of their lives, makes it seem unreal to me. I really can't believe that something like this can happen in the world without a bigger outcry about it. It really hurts me, again, like it has hurt me in the past, to witness how awful we can allow the world to be. I felt after talking to you that maybe you didn't completely believe me. I think it's actually good if you don't, because I do believe pretty much above all in the importance of independent critical thinking ... [But] I am witnessing this chronic, insidious genocide and I'm really scared, and questioning my fundamental belief in the goodness of human nature. This has to stop. I think it is a good idea for us all to drop everything and devote our lives to making this stop.

Few adults see with the clarity of one so young—one whose truth arouses such fear that the barbarians must silence her forever. After taking her life, some have continued silencing her in death by banning her words from theater. Had she returned alive she said she would have returned wounded, as a veteran soldier is psychologically wounded with post traumatic stress. "When I come back from Palestine," she logged in her journal, "I probably will have nightmares and constantly feel guilty for not being here, but I can channel that into more work. Coming here is one of the better things I've ever done. So when I sound crazy, or if the Israeli military should break with their racist tendency not to injure white people, please pin the reason squarely on the fact that I am in the midst of a genocide which I am also indirectly supporting, and for which my government is largely responsible." Few people ever become as liberated in struggle as to summon a powerful courage sufficient to confront man's brutality, his crimes against humanity. Rachel Corrie did. And while her dying brought no bold headlines or flags of mourning, her life stands in the struggle, in the truth of women as makers of peace.

Some people inherit their lives and let their inheritance destroy them. Others take the inheritance and rise up on it. If their lives are prolific in work, they lift thousands. Alice Walker is prolific—in the poetry of her activist life.

Author *Alice Walker* was born among Deep South sharecroppers but instead of negating sharecropping she leans into it, embraces it and teases strength out of the sharecropper. The human spirit has the power to purge bitterness from pain she writes in her book *In Search of Our Mothers' Gardens*. Southern black sharecroppers and poor farmers took a religion intended to pacify them into accepting their enslavement and transformed it into an antidote against bitterness. "Depending on one another, because they had nothing and no one else, the sharecropper often managed to come through 'all right.'"

How we come to be "all right" comes from where we came from and how we came through the tough stuff. Walker returns to this strength in a 1970 piece, "The Black Writer and the Southern Experience." She writes: "In large measure, black Southern writers owe their clarity of vision to parents who refused to diminish themselves as human beings by succumbing to racism. Our parents seemed to know that an extreme negative emotion held against other human beings for reasons they do not control can be blinding. Blindness about other human beings, especially for a writer, is equivalent to death."

Continually Walker returns to the motif *liberation in struggle, struggle that liberates,* and what a person does with *inheritance.* The Southern writer is special heir, owing special responsibility, Walker writes. "No one could wish for a more advantageous heritage than that bequeathed to the black writer in the South: a compassion for the earth, a trust in humanity beyond our knowledge of evil, and an abiding love of justice. We inherit a great responsibility as well, for we must give voice to centuries not only of silent bitterness and hate but also of neighborly kindness and sustaining love."

Work itself is a struggle that liberates. Focus is critical. In an interview with *Democracy Now*'s Amy Goodman, Walker said, "[When] you are working on your work, you really don't have to be concerned about what other people are doing. At some point, if your work is as true as you can make it, it has its own luminosity and it inevitably brings to you and your work all the people that you need."

Alice Walker revived Harlem Renaissance writer-storyteller Zora Neale Hurston and later watched her own award-winning book *The Color Purple* adapted for screen in the 1980s and in 2005 staged on Broadway. When asked in 2006 to summarize *The Color Purple*'s message, Walker returns to *struggle as liberation.*

> I feel that when you read *The Color Purple,* no matter what is happening in your life or how difficult the whole huge miasma of sorrow that seems to be growing, there's a way that you can see through the life of Celie [main female character]: That if you can continue and if you can stay connected to nature and also to your highest sense of behavior toward yourself and toward other people, if you can really keep that struggle going ... [though] ... life can be really hard, people can abuse you, ... take advantage of you in terrible ways, but there is something in the human spirit that's actually equal to that and can actually overcome ...

From its December 1, 2005, opening, Alice Malsenior Walker's *The Color Purple* played to sold-out Broadway audiences. Walker's writing career extends decades and includes novels and essays, poetry and short story collections. Among them *In Search of Our Mothers' Gardens; Revolutionary Petunias and Other Poems; Good Night Willie Lee, I'll see you in the Morning; In Love and Trouble: Stories of Black Women; You Can't Keep a Good Woman Down.* Her novels include *Meridian, The Color Purple, The Temple of My Familiar*, and *Now Is the Time to Open Your Heart.* Walker has been called an activist and visionary. She has participated in "most of the major movements of planetary change": Hands off Cuba, women's rights, Native American and indigenous rights, free South Africa, environmental, animal rights and peace movements; human and civil rights movements of the United States South. In her interview with Amy Goodman, Alice Walker said, "No matter what people are slinging at you, no mater what is happening, life itself, basic life is incredibly precious."

Rachel Corrie and Alice Walker, Mary Ann Wright and Cindy Sheehan, women Nobel Laureates, and workers from the wilderness share a spiritual bond: the struggle. They are makers of peace whose work and words are altering world order.

"You cannot shake hands with clenched fists."

Four-term (1966–77; 1980–1984) Prime Minister of India, Indira Priyad Arshini Gandhi (b. 1917, d. 1984)

Afterword

An Idea whose Time Has Come

Eighty years have passed since the people ratified woman's right to vote and enshrined that right in the Constitution of the United States of America. At the start of the twenty-first century women's numbers in population and work (inside and outside their homes) exceeded men's numbers in work and population—and there is every reason to believe these trends will continue. Yet in all the years and struggle from Woman Suffrage forward, the U.S. electorate has failed to seat a single woman in the first chair of federal government's highest elective executive office. Since the Second World War male dominance increasingly has led with a belligerent foreign policy, one after another undeclared war (often simultaneous wars), leaving in its wake a domestic policy of neglect, class conflict, chasms among people. This manner of being—further corrupted by corporate billions bankrolling public officials and the mass media who cover them—has caused the "leader of the free world" to regress, to move backward, seeming to render itself incapable of ceding top executive government leadership to a woman. However the poet rejoins in noting that invasions "of armies can be resisted but not an idea whose time has come."

This first ever international, multiethnic, multiracial guide and notebook seeking to move readers out of the narrow politics of spin and inhumanity of men and into a better world order—as seen thorough a uniquely drawn selection of government, press, and activist women's words and work—is grounded also in a (*feminist?*) set of ideas.

> Substantive work and words of women on and off center stage are essential to the world. *Woman's difference* in action makes a crucial difference in world affairs.

Revealed in thoughts, speeches, feelings, discussions and debates, in writings and activism, *woman's difference* must be ferreted out and taken to heart, taken seriously (at least as seriously as man's voice), by generations of women (and men).

The voices of change makers, such as those profiled, quoted and commented on in this book, particularly those concerned with justice, nonviolence, free press, and peaceful coexistence must be uncensored: aired equally with the men in print, broadcast and other forms of mass media.

Women's contributions to ending poverty and violence, protecting the environment, ensuring justice under law and other world challenges as covered in *Women's Work and Words Altering World Order* must be uncovered.

Through the provision of clean democratic processes, women's advancement to top-tier executive, judicial, and legislative leadership must be unimpeded.

The leader of the free world needs a woman head of state—but a particular woman—with the intellect and presence of mind to ponder action with an eye to the future; a human-centeredness capable of respecting difference and envisioning peaceful cooperation and coexistence with and among nations; a woman unconcerned with showing how tough she is, or how religious she is, or how fashion-setting her wardrobe.

References: Sources, Background, Cited Works

Women's Work and Words Altering World Order: Alternatives to Spin and Inhumanity of Men (notes and commentary on nonviolence, justice, change makers, peaceful coexistence) has been adapted from ideas in the author's news and current affairs columns but is an entirely new work containing new profiles, excerpts from political speeches, statistics on worldwide women heads of state and legislators, women-sponsored anti-war legislation, news quotes and interviews, and other new material tied in with the author's running commentary.

I. Women Crossing Continents Crossing Borders Crossing Colors

Women's Work and Words in the Spirit of International Women's Day
Rider from Wrong Side of Tracks in Olson's *Freedom's Daughters*

Summers, Barbara, ed. 1989. *I Dream a World*. New York: Stewart, Tabori & Chang.

Hine, Darlene, Elsa Brown, and Rosalyn Terborg-Penn, eds. 1993. Joycelyn Elders, Mary Ann Shadd Cary. In *Black Women in America: An Historical Encyclopedia*. Bloomington: Indiana University Press.

Olson, Lynne. 2002. *Freedom's Daughters: The Unsung Heroines of the Civil Rights Movement from 1830-1970*. New York: Simon and Schuster.

Bennett, Carolyn. March 8, 2003. "International Women's Day, National Women's History Month: Take Action."

De Lu, Darien. January 2003. "On Disarming Despair." *Peace and Freedom Magazine*. Women's International League for Peace and Freedom: www.wilpf.org.

Bennett, Carolyn. February 18, 2004. "African-American History Month Remembers Women's Legacies."

Bennett, Carolyn. November 1, 2005. "Claudette Colvin's Civil Rights Contribution Censored Favoring Rosa Parks: Correcting a Civil Rights Record."

Bennett, Carolyn. November 2, 2005. "Olson's *Freedom's Daughters.*"

II. Women Refusing to Stand Idly By

Women's Words and Work Ending Violence against Children, Women

Madonna, Josephine Baker and Children

Millender-McDonald and Women

Children

Bennett, Carolyn. November 8, 2006. "Venturing into Humanness Saves World's Children: Josephine to Madonna" Also cited in article: http://news. bbc.co.uk/; http://web1.infotrac.galegroup.com/. Reuters AlertNet http:// www.alertnet.org/. http://www.avert.org/worldstats.htm; London-based Campaign Against Arms Trade (CAAT); United Nations reports."The Josephine Baker Story." HBO film, 1991. Http://www.cwgl.rutgers.edu. **mailto:cwgl@igc.org**

Women, Children (USA)

Bennett, Carolyn. December 1, 2001. "Carol Bellamy Standing by Children: Women No Longer Stand Idly By." Cited in article: http://www. indiancountry.com; http://www.iht.com; http://www.amnestyusa.org/ stopviolence/takaction.html; http://www.amnestyusa.org/women;

http://www.nyc.gov/html/doh/pdf/ip/femicide1995-2002_report.pdf; htttp://www.womenscommission.org.

Bennett, Carolyn. January 28, 2004. "Rape in a Georgia Town."

Bennett, Carolyn. November 10, 2004. "Sixteen Days' activism End Violence against Women."

Millender-McDonald, Juanita. February 7, 2002. "Preventing Violence against Women" Floor Remarks, U.S. House of Representatives. In Iowa

State University Archive of Women's Political Communication—The Carrie Chapman Catt Center: http://www.womenspeecharchive.org/women/profile/speech/index.cfm?ProfileID=45&SpeechID=181; http://infotrac.galegroup.com

Women (World)

[United Nations High Commissioner for Refugees: http://www.unhcr.org

"Declaration on the Elimination of Violence against Women." General Assembly Resolution 48/1041 (1993, December 20).

Bennett, Carolyn. December 20, 2001. "Men Making Chattel of Children: Women must No Longer Stand Idly By."

Sargand, Payenda December 7, 2006. "Pain of Afghan Suicide Women." http://news.bbc.co.uk.

Penketh, Anne. March 8, 2007 "Struggle for Equality and Freedom in Developing Countries" [focus: women and girls]. The *Independent*, UK.

Guernica Magazine "First Victims of Freedom" Interview with Iraqi Feminist Yanar Mohammed. http://www.guernicamag.com/interviews/326/the_black_glove (2007, May).

Fang, Bay. "Women under Attack: The Talibanization of Iraq" (Ms Magazine). http://www.alternet.org/story/51621/(2007, May 9).

Toensing, Gale. May 18, 2005. "Sexual Violence against Indigenous Women Discussed at United Nations. *Indian Country Today*.

III. Women Practicing Journalism under Fire

Daisy Bates

Anna Politkovskaya

Killed, Kidnapped, Jailed, Wounded

Giuliana Sgrena

Bates, Daisy. 1962. *The Long Shadow of Little Rock*. New York: David McKay Co.

Bennett, Carolyn. November 6, 1999. "A Daisy to Remember."

Bennett, Carolyn. May 12, 2004. "Diversity Resistant Press Resists Democracy."

Bennett, Carolyn. February 23, 2005. "Gentlemen of the Press."

Economist. October 14, 2006. "Anna Politkovskaya, a Russian Journalist, was shot dead on October 7th, aged 48."

Bennett, Carolyn. October 8, 2006. Comment on death of Anna Politkovskaya.

Bennett, Carolyn. October 18, 2006. "Dying doing it: Women Must Continue Practicing Journalism in Public Interest." Sources in article: Committee to Protect Journalists: http://www.cpj.org./killed/killed_ archives/stats.html; Reporters without Borders http://www.rsf.org; http:// www.socialistworker.co.uk/

Bennett, Carolyn. February 19, 2007. Giuliana Sgrena's *Friendly Fire*: War Fails to Silence Witnesses Urging Withdrawal.

Sgrena, Giuliana. (2006) *Friendly Fire: The remarkable story of a journalist kidnaped in Iraq, rescued by an Italian secret service agent, and shot by U.S. forces* authored by Giuliana Sgrena with English translation by Lesley Freeman Riva, editing by William Keach, foreword by Amy Goodman and Denis Moynihan: First published in the United States in 2006 by Haymarket Books; First published in France in 2005 by Giangiacomo Feltrinelli. The book is highly recommended for insights into the Middle East; war and its impact on journalists and journalism, truth and societies; Iraq and Iraqis, interrelations among sects, factions, Iranians, Internationals; abduction; friendly fire; impunity; and reasons for withdrawal and reconstruction.

Economist (April 7, 2007. "A Slice of Death." [Review of the book *A Russian Diary* By Anna Politkovskaya]

AlJazeera English. June 7, 2007. "Gaza's Women Journalists Threatened."

Cockburn, Patrick. June 12, 2007. "Murder highlights death toll of Iraqi Journalists." *Independent*. http://news.independent.co.uk/world/middle_east.

IV. Women Judges, Lawyers upholding United States Constitution

Diana Gribbon Motz, Ruth Bader Ginsburg, Gladys Kessler

Constance Baker Motley

Lani Guinier Empowered by Motley

Words and Work: Women Jurists, Lawyers from Harvard

Motley, Constance. 1998. *Equal Justice under Law: An Autobiography*. New York: Farrar, Straus, & Giroux.

Harvard Bulletin. Spring 1999. "Lani Guinier: Present and Visible."

Guinier, Lani. December 4, 2000. "Making Every Vote Count." The *Nation*: http://www.thenation.com/.

Harvard Bulletin. Summer 2003. "Nifty 50: Women Graduates of Harvard Now Practicing Lawyers and Judges." http://www.law.harvard.edu/alumni/bulletin/2003/summer/feature_5-1.html.

Bennett, Carolyn. October 5, 2005. "Constance Baker Motley's Sense of Self, Duty: Our Sense of Self, Duty." Also [excerpted from Motley's 1998 book *Equal Justice Under Law* at http://partners.nytimes.com/books/first/m/motley-equal.html].

Inside Higher Education. February 8, 2007. "Tobacco on Trial in California." [August 2006 ruling that ended a multi-year federal racketeering and fraud lawsuit against nine tobacco companies, Judge Gladys Kessler criticized tobacco companies for manipulating science to fit claims that tobacco is harmless."] http://www.insidehighered.com.

"Court Upholds Military Proceedings for Detainees" [In a 2-1 decision the Appeals]. February 20, 2007. Narr. Ari Shapiro. NPR: All Things Considered. [Judge Judith Rogers dissented. In her dissent she said the court had misread the historical record and ignored the Supreme Court].

550 U. S.__ (2007)—Ginsburg, J., dissenting. Supreme Court of the United States. No. 05-1074. Lilly M. Ledbetter Petitioner v. The Goodyear Tire & Rubber Company Inc. On Writ of Certiorari to the United States

Court of Appeals for the Eleventh Circuit, May 29, 2007. http://www.supremecourtus.gov/opinions/06pdf/05-1074.pdf.

Leonnig, Carol. June 12, 2007. "Judges Rule Against U.S. On Detained 'Combatant'." *Washington Post*: http://www.washingtonpost.com.

Richey, Warren. June 12, 2007. "War on Terror Error." Chicago Sun *Times*: http://www.suntimes.com. [In a 2-1 ruling the federal appeals court said: "U.S. residents cannot be held without charges." Judge Diana Gribbon Motz wrote: "To sanction such presidential authority to order the military to seize and indefinitely detain civilians, even if the president calls them 'enemy combatants,' would have disastrous consequences for the Constitution."

Associated Press. July 20, 2007. "Court: Judges Need All Detainee Evidence." *Guardian*.

"The U.S. Court of Appeals for the District of Columbia Circuit rejected [unanimously] the Bush administration's plan to limit what judges and the detainees' attorneys can review when considering whether the Combatant Status Review Tribunals acted appropriately: Counsel for a detainee has a 'need to know' the classified information relating to his client's case.'" [Judge Judith Rogers sits on this court.] http://www.guardian.co.uk/worldlatest/story/.

V. U.S. Women Policymakers, Lawmakers, Peacemakers

Past to Present (Barbara Jordan, National Unity)

Eligible 2007 for U. S. Presidency

(Photo layout)

Eligible But Can They Afford the Admission Price?

Bennett, Carolyn. May 28, 2007. "Memorial Day 2007 Remembering Common Destiny, National Unity."

[Barbara Jordan] http://www.AmericanRhetoric.com.

Bennett, Carolyn. March 9, 2005. "Lengthening List of Women Candidates for U.S. Presidency."

Bennett, Carolyn. November 16, 2005. "Powerful Women Prostituting away their Power (Rice, Miers, Karpinski, Clinton, Lewinsky)." Also sources: http://www.beaufortgazette.com/local_news; http://www.sptimes.com; http://books.gaurdian.co.uk; http://www.democracy.org.

Schroeder, Patricia. 1998. *24 years of Housework … and the Place is Still a Mess: My Life in Politics.* Kansas City, Missouri: Andrews McMeel Publishing.

Bennett, Carolyn. February 15, 2002. "Join Congresswomen in Campaign Finance Reform."

Reuters. May 5, 2007. "U.S. System Trips up Women Seeking Presidency."

Open Secrets. June 19, 2007. "The Big Picture 2005 Cycle: The Price of Admission," "How does the wealth primary work: The Prohibitive Price of Admission," "The Wealth Primary as the Key to Victory," "Campaign Finance Reform," "The Rising Prices of Victory: Most and Least Expensive Winning Senate Campaigns." Center for Responsive Politics. http://www.opensecrets.org.

"Women in Statewide Elective Executive Office 2007." Center for American Women and Politics, Eagleton Institute of Politics, Rutgers, The State University of New Jersey, 191 Ryders Lane, New Brunswick, NJ 08901-8557, (732) 932-9384—Fax: (732) 932-0014. http://www.cawp.rutgers.edu.

Christensen, Martin. June 1, 2007. Current Women Leaders Worldwide Guide to Women in Leadership: Women Heads of State. www.guide2womenleaders.com.

Deutsche Welle. August 3, 2007. "UN Report Good and Bad News for Working Women." www.dw-world.de.

VI. U. S. Women Credentialed but Off Center Stage

Kathleen Sebelius (Kansas Governor)

Shirley Chisholm ("Candidate of the People")

Woolsey & Lee (Peace, Justice Duo in Congress)

Wright & Sheehan (Camp Casey, Anti-war)

Woolsey, Lee, Waters (Bring them Home)

South Central LA: Maxine Waters

In Memoriam: Juanita Millender-McDonald

Chisholm, Shirley. 1973. *The Good Fight*. New York: Harper & Row.

Chisholm, Shirley. 1970. *Unbought and Unbossed*. Boston: Houghton Mifflin.

Bennett, Carolyn. January 5, 2005. "To the Democratic Party from Shirley Chisholm."

Bennett, Carolyn. September 23, 2001. "My Kind of Patriot."

Bennett, Carolyn. March 25, 2007. "Applaud Lee, Waters, Woolsey's Courage." Article cites:

http://thomas.loc.gov/cgi-bin/bdquery/z?d109:h.con.res.00035;   http:// woolsey.house.gov/latestnews;   http://www.lee.house.gov;   http://waters. house.gov

http://www.govexec.com/.

"Women in the Senate." Senate Historical Office. www.senate.gov.

Lee, Barbara. March 23, 2007. "Barbara Lee's Statement on the Passage of the Iraq Accountability Act." http://lee.house.gov.

Lee, Barbara March 8, 2007. Barbara Lee and Colleagues Unveil Plan to Fully Fund Withdrawal of U.S. Troops from Iraq." http://lee.house.gov.

Bennett, Carolyn. November 22, 2006. "Pelosi Knows Peace begins with the Women." Also sources: http://holt.house.gov/pdf/CRS_on_women_ in_Congress_Sep_2005.pdf;   http://www.house.gov/;   http://woolsey. house.gov/;   http://lee.house.gov/;   http://thomas.loc.gov/;   http://www. alaskareport.com;   http://www.nytimes.com;   http://msnbs.com;   http:// www.baltimoresun.com;   http://www.citizensforethics.org;   http://galenet. galegroup.com/servlet/BioRC. The *Economist* (2006, November 4). "Madam Speaker?"

Millender-McDonald, Juanita. December 21, 2001. "Strengthen Social Security" Floor Statement, U.S. House of Representatives. In Iowa

State University Archive of Women's Political Communication—The Carrie Chapman Catt Center: Millender-McDonald speeches: Social Security and the Bush/Republican Privatization plans. http://www. womenspeechesarchive.org/women/profile/speech/index.cfm?ProfileID=4 5&SpeechID=181. Also http://infotrac.galegroup.com

Millender-McDonald, Juanita. April 6, 2002. "Expanding the Reach." Women's Empowerment Conference: Los Angeles. In Iowa State University Archive of Women's Political Communication—The Carrie Chapman Catt Center: Millender-McDonald speeches http://www.womenspeechesarchive. org/women/profile/speech/index.

Bennett, Carolyn. April 12, 2006. "Missing in Immigration Debate, Rep. Sheila Jackson-Lee's Bill." Also: "Rep. Sheila Jackson lee: Immigration is the Civil Right Issue of our Time." April 4, 2006. Democracy Now. http:// www.democracynow.org.

Sebelius, Kathleen. January 10, 2007. "Kansas Tomorrow: Fulfilling Our Promise."

Governor Kathleen Sebelius' State of the State Address.

In Anti-war Movement

Bennett, Carolyn. November 23, 2005. "Powerful Women Sacrificing to Bring them Home. Also: http://www.atimes.com); (http://thomas.loc.gov/ cgi-bin/bdquery/z?d109:h.con.res.00035);

http://woolsey.house.gov/latestnews;   http://www.lee.house.gov;   http:// www.govexec.com/;

http://www.swingthevote.us/wright.html;   (excerpt   from   http://www. dailykos.com/storyonly/2007/5/28/12530/1525)

Skons, Elisabeth. 2007. Military Expenditure (Chapter 8). In Yearbook A World at Risk. Stockholm International Peace Research Institute, Chapter 8. http://www.sipri.org

VII. World Women Policymakers, Lawmakers, Peacemakers

Five Leading Change Makers in Words and Work

Hanan Ashrawi (Middle East)

Wangari Maathai (East Africa)

Angela Merkel (Germany)

Helen Caldicott (Australia/United States of America)

Mary McAleese (Ireland)

Merkel, Angela. January 24, 2007. "Opening Address by Angela Merkel, Chancellor or the Federal Republic of Germany, at the World Economic Forum in Davos" (transcript-translation).

McAleese, Mary. February 15, 2006. "Address by the President of Ireland, Mary McAleese, to a joint meeting of the Houses of the Jordanian Parliament, Amman." http://www.president.ie/index.php?section=5&speech=214&lang=eng.

Merkel, Angela. March 25, 2007. "Speech by Dr. Angela Merkel, Chancellor of the Federal Republic of Germany and President of the European Council, at the official ceremony to celebrate the 50th anniversary of the signing of the Treaties of Rome." http://www.eu2007.de.en/News/Speeches.

Caldicott, Helen. "Credo." Nuclear Policy Research Institute Creating Consensus for a Nuclear-Free Future. http://www.nuclearpolicy.org

Breakfast with David Frost. October 15, 2000. Hanan Ashrawi Interview (transcript). British Broadcasting Corporation.

Breakfast with David Frost. September 16, 2001. Former Israeli Prime Minister Benjamin Netanyahu, Palestinian Legislative Council Member Hanan Ashrawi Interview (transcript): British Broadcasting Corporation.

Your World Today. November 15, 2005. U.S. Secretary of State Condoleezza Rice, Palestinian Legislator Hanan Ashrawi on News: "Gaza Deal Reached"; "U.S. Senate Defeats Proposal to Set Timetable for Withdrawing U.S. Troops from Iraq." Interview (transcript). Correspondents Zain Verjee, Michael Holmes, Guy Raz Interview. Cable News Network International.

Steinfels, Margaret. June 16, 1995. "The Woman Behind the Scenes. (Palestinian Peace Negotiator Hanan Ashrawi." Commonweal. [References "This Side of Peace: A Personal Account" by Hanan Ashrawi].

Democracy Now. October 8, 2004. "Kenyan Environmentalist Wangari Maathai Wins Nobel Peace Prize." Terry Tempest Williams Interview (transcript). Amy Goodman. http://www.democracynow.org.

Maathai, Wangari. 2007. *Unbowed: A Memoir*. New York: Knoph Publishing Group (paperback release).

Baltimore Times. March 23, 2007. "Women's History Month Profile in Courage: Dr. Wangari Maathai."

Norwegian Nobel Institute: http://nobelpeaceprize.org.

VIII. Women Political Decision Makers Worldwide

World Women Heads of State (non-monarchs)

World Women's Percentages: High Legislative, Executive Government 2007

Bari, Farzana. November 3, 2005. "Women's Political Participation: Issues and Challenges." United Nations Division for the Advancement of Women.

Christensen, Martin. June 1, 2007. Current Women Leaders Worldwide Guide to Women in Leadership: Women Heads of State. www.guide2womenleaders.com

"Women in Statewide Elective Executive Office 2007." Center for American Women and Politics, Eagleton Institute of Politics, Rutgers, The State University of New Jersey, 191 Ryders Lane, New Brunswick, NJ 08901-8557, (732) 932-9384—Fax: (732) 932-0014. http://www.cawp.rutgers.edu

International

Bennett, Carolyn. March 8, 2006. "International Women's vision Teaches Americans." Also sources: http://www.mofa/gov.bd/bimstec/om_speech.html; Prime Minister Begum Kaleda Zia, People's Republic of Bangladesh; Latvian President Vike-Freiberga: http://www.president.lv/index/; GlobeWomen.com; New Zealand Prime Minister Helen Elizabeth Clark: http://www.beehive.govt.nz/; Ireland President Mary McAleese: http://

www.president.ie/index; Finland President Tarja Halonen: http://www.president.fi/netcomm/news; German Chancellor Angela Merkel: www.globalmarshallplan.org.; France, Jamaica, Philippine, Sao Tome & Principe Women heads of state and contenders: http://news.scotsman.com/politics.

IX. Briefly Noted Words

Ellen Johnson-Sirleaf (Liberia)

Angela Merkel (Germany)

Michelle Bachelet (Chile)

Tarja Halonen (Finland)

Wangari Maathai (Kenya)

Christine Gregoire (USA)

Segolene Royal (France)

Lynda Lovejoy (Navajo Nation)

Rigoberta Menchu (Guatemala)

Odette Nyiramilimo (Rwanda)

Rwanda

Goering, Laurie. September 3, 2006. "Female Leaders boost Rwanda's Social Progress; 12 years after genocide, world's highest percentage of female legislators push for equality." *The Houston Chronicle*.

Goering. Laurie. April 2004, Kigali, Rwanda. "From Africa Recovery, Women break into African politics"; Gumisai Mutume: Quota systems allow more women to gain elected office."

France

Hussey, Andrew. July 23, 2006. "Is France Ready for a Woman President?" *Guardian*: http://www.guardian.co.uk.

Lichfield, John. April 23, 2007. "Sarkozy and Royal go through as 84 percent turnout sets new poll record." The *Independent*: http://news.independent.co.uk/europe/.

Bretton, Laure. November 16, 2006. "France's Royal Wins Socialist Vote, Eyes 2007." *Reuters*.

Gehmlich, Kerstin and Francois Murphy. February 19, 2007. "France's Royal says faces more attacks than a man." *Reuters*.

Germany

Deutsche Welle. April 1, 2007. "Seize the Moment for Peace, Merkel Urges Middle East." http://www.dw-world.de.

Deutsche Welle March 1, 2007. "German Chancellor Call EU to Tackle Global Challenges."

Economist January 13, 2007. "Tricky weather: Germany's Role in Europe is Changing." [Chancellor Angela Merkel].

Native American

Fonseca, Felicia. August 9, 2006. "Navajo Woman to be First to Run Tribal Presidency." (AP) http://www.freenewmexican.com/story.

http://seatlepi.nwsource.com; http://www.navajo.org; http://www.nativetimes. com

India

Singh, Jyotsna. July 24, 2007. "Indian Women Politicians on Rise." http://news.bbc.co.uk.

British Broadcasting. July 21, 2007. Profile: Pratibha Patil. Http://news.bbc.co.uk.

AlJazeera English July 21, 2007. "India Elects First Woman President." http://english.aljazeera.net/News/.

Liberia

Deutsche Welle. January 16, 2007. "Liberian Government in Office One Year." [President Ellen Johnson-Sirleaf]

Chile

BBC October 15, 2006. "Chile Head Revisits Torture Site." [President Michelle Bachelet]

USA

Economist August 5, 2006. "Recovering from a Bitter Victory." [Washington State governor Christine Gregoire].

X. World Peace Women Altering World Order

Nobel Women

Global Women

Women from the Wilderness:

Women's International League for Peace and Freedom to Iraqi Women

Ann Wright, Cindy Sheehan

Rachel Corrie, Alice Walker

Bennett, Carolyn.. October 6, 2001. "Voices of Peace, Voices of Patriotism."

Bennett, Carolyn. December 14, 2001. "Nobel Peace and Women." Also sources: http://www.nobelwomensinitiative.org

Bennett, Carolyn. February 8, 2003. "Voices of Peace from Shortwave." Also sources: http://www.rfpi.org; http://www.nonviolence.org/vitw; http://www.votenowar.org/referendum.html; http://www.votetoimpeach.org; http://www.democracynow.org; www.wilpf.org; http://www.indymedia.org.

Bennett, Carolyn. March 22, 2003. "Rachel Corrie of Olympia ... exposing Barbarity of War."

Bennett, Carolyn. October 14, 2003. "This Year's Nobel Peace Laureate sends Message to America." [Shirin Ebadi].

Ruffin, Fayth. June-August, 2004. "Women as Peacemakers (10 Stories the World Should Hear More About." UN *Chronicle.*

Bennett, Carolyn. November 23, 2005. "Powerful Women Sacrificing to Bring them Home."

Bennett, Carolyn. March 1, 2006. "Winter Celebration of Hope in the Life and Words of Alice Walker."

Economist. September 23, 2006. "African Greenheart: Conservation and Feminism." [Review of the book Unbowed: A Memoir by Wangari Maathai].

Bennett, Carolyn. December 20, 2006. "Peace Makers Urge Care for underlying Causes, Multi-lateral Means to Peace." Also sources: http://news. bbc.co.uk; **http://news.bbc.co.uk;**http://www.nobelwomensinitiative.org; http://www.un.org; http://www.globalfundforwomen.org; http://nobelprize. org; http://www.grameen-info. org http://www.juancole. com/2006/11/233-dead-in-civil-war-carnage-health. html; http://www.kucinich.us/; http://www. democracynow.org/

Bennett, Carolyn. January 29, 2007. Price of Liberty: "Right and Duty to Protest War Vigilantly with a Sense of History."

Memarian, Omid. April 25, 2007. "Iran: Nobel Peace Laureate Calls for Nuclear Referendum." Inter Press Service News Agency.

Bennett, Carolyn. May 29, 2007. "Excerpted from Cindy Sheehan's Memorial Morning Missive to America."

Norwegian Nobel Institute: http://nobelpeaceprize.org.

Preface
The Case for New Ethos

Afterword
An Idea whose Time Has Come

In Current Affairs Syndicated Columns

Bennett, Carolyn. (2005, August 17). "Sabers Rattling Toward Iran: Missing Context."

_____. (2005, August 31). "Bush's War against Us and the World."

_____. (2005, September 21). "United Nations at 60: the Powerful Few Promote Poverty."

_____. (2005, October 26). "Saddam's Atrocities, and Ours."

_____. (2006, February 1). "Why you should Care about this Surveillance."

_____. (2006, February 9). "Unspoken State of Union."

_____. (2006, February 22). "Outlaw Government."

_____. (2006, March 15). "Nuclear Proliferation: America's Self-Inflicting Threat."

_____. (2006, April 19). "Religionists Create False Security in War."

_____. (2006, May 17). "U.S. Threatens Return to Cole War, Dismisses Historic Letter."

_____. (2006, May 24). "Second Greatest Threat: A New McCarthyism."

_____. (2006, June 7). "Trail of Tears to Haditha—Americans' Dark Side."

_____. (2006, August 9). "Carnage in Middle East Begs Honest Peacemaker."

_____. (2006, August 28). "Constitutional Movements Forced from imperial Executive."

_____. (2006, October 3). "World Refugees: Nations' World Wars, Unaffordable Migrations."

_____. (2006, October 23). "Bush Breaches Universal Declaration of Human Rights."

_____. (2006, November 13). "Another Unindicted Co-Conspirator: Iran-Contra Figure Nominated to Head DOD."

_____. (2006, December 4). "Narrow, *Racialized* Vision Hiding National, World Tragedies."

_____. (2006, December 11). "U.S. Kills own people, thousands of Iraqis to Continue Appropriating Middle Eastern Oil."

_____. (2007, February 5). "One Nation Under Violence Divisible, Destructive."

_____. (2007, February 12). "Human Rights Abuse, Friendly Fire, Corruption: The Matter of U.S. Impunity and Backlash."

_____. (2007, February 26). "Unchecked Power, Crimes Against Universe: Unacceptable in Nature—Power Ridding Itself of its Unwanted—Dumping."

_____. (2007, March 5). "Status Quo—the Read Evil Axis."

_____. (2007, March 12). "China's Human Rights Report on America."

_____. (2007, March 19). "Missile Shield Prevents Peace, Divides Peoples, Spawns New Cold War."

_____. (2007, March 26). "Allies, Patriots' Hard Truths urge Washington to Mend its Ways."

_____. (2007, April 2). "Force on Ground Belies Feigned Shock: U.S. Again at War."

_____. (2007, May 5). "Pleasure to the Chief is Poisoning Everybody Else."

_____. (2007, April 16). "U.S. Government expands Aggression while Media Feed Feud."

_____. (2007, May 12). "Inbred, Monolithic Power: As Blair Leaves, Notes on U.S. Legacy"

_____. (2007, June 15). "Raw Power Piercing the Heart."

_____. (2007, June 22). "Muddle Middle Fails leadership World Needs."

About the Author

At the height of the 1970s Women's Rights Movement in the United States, Dr. Carolyn LaDelle Bennett returned from the National Women's Conference at Houston, Texas, to publish women's voices and achievements in a small newspaper she founded, the *Network of North Carolina Women*. In later years she taught courses in print journalism and public affairs at Howard University, the University of Maine, and other colleges. She has been writing a news and current affairs column for alternative weeklies and a variety of magazines for at least a generation. Among her earlier books are *Missing News and Views in Paranoid Times*, *Talking Back to Today's News*, and *America's Human Connection: Commentary on Us*. She's a nonpartisan, independent journalist living and writing in New York State.

Some of the Internet Web Sites Carrying or Citing Bennett's Writings

http://www.greenbeltmovement.org/a.php?id=52

http://commentisfree.guardian.co.uk/katrina_vanden_heuvel/2006/10/katrina.html

http://www.wifp.org/AssociateWebsites.html

http://movies.aol.com/movie/the-queen-2006/24070/reviews-critic

http://www2.xlibris.com/bookstore/author.asp?authorid=18273

http://www.exodusnews.com/editorials/editorial-127.html

http://journals.aol.com/cwriter85/TodaysMissingNews/

http://www.commondreams.org/views01/1220-06.htm

http://peacecorpswriters.org/pages/depts/archives/journalsofpeace/jp21st0345pm.html

http://www.mellenpress.com/mellenpress.cfm?aid=475&pc=10

http://digitalcommons.unl.edu/pocpwi4/

hometown.aol.com/cwriter85/index.html—168k

http://www.greatwomen.org/women.php?action=viewone&id=18

http://www.amazon.co.jp/Talking-Today%C2%AAs-Carolyn-LaDelle-Bennett/dp/1592868215

http://findarticles.com/p/search?tb=art&qt=%22Mary+McLeod+Bethune%22&sn=10

http://www.amazon.com/s?ie=UTF8&index=books&field-keywords=Bethune%2C%20Mary%20McLeod&page=1

http://www.amazon.co.uk/s?ie=UTF8&keywords=Public%20Affairs%20%26%20Administration&rh=n%3A62%2Ck%3APublic%20Affairs%20%26%20Administration&page=1

167

http://www.amazon.ca/s?ie=UTF8&keywords=1945-1953&rh=n%3A95 2366%2Ck%3A1945-1953&page=1

http://www.worldcatlibraries.org/wcpa/top3mset/44594056

http://www.opengroup.com/books/index/bkbsv800.shtml

http://www.amazon.fr/s?ie=UTF8&keywords=Public%20Affairs%20%26 %20Administration&rh=n%3A81604011%2Ck%3APublic%20Affairs% 20%26%20Administration&page=1

http://www.ecampus.com/isbnbrowser2/isbnstart/15928

http://www.omnicenter.org/omniprojects/bib24.html

Subjects Index

Names Index

Page numbers in italics indicate a photograph

978-0-595-46712-9
0-595-46712-1